Femdom Academy

SM Course for Mistresses & Subs,

Beginners & Advanced.

By Lady Sas.

Frankfurt/Main, February 2021

Updated August 2023

Content

Notice:

The author accepts no liability for any physical or psychological harm that may result from the SM practices described in this book. The responsibility for the safe and responsible practice of BDSM remains with the reader.

Foreword

Welcome, dear reader. I invite you: Come with me on an exciting and varied journey into the fascinating world of BDSM. Into a world filled with wild imaginations, bizarre experiences, sexual pleasure, and joy.

This book is aimed at Femdoms and subs, singles and couples, beginners and advanced learners, who are looking for a contemporary course and guide to BDSM. The title "Femdom Academy" suggests that we will look at things from the perspective of the mistress. However, male subs will also learn everything they need to know while reading the book. They will probably even learn to understand their Mistress better this way.

Since the *50 Shades of Grey* phenomenon, almost every sexually open-minded person probably has some basic idea of BDSM. For this reason, I didn't want to design a course aimed only at beginners. The danger of boring my readers because they already know everything was too great for me. That's why this course goes far beyond the basics. We talk about it - but we also go much further. I have tried to write the book in such a way that it helps both beginners and advanced learners and is fun at the same time.

Now you are probably already curious about what awaits you. So, here we go! I hope you enjoy reading this book.

Cordially,

Lady Sas

PS: BDSM is a separate world with its own terms. I have therefore included a glossary in the appendix where I explain the most important technical terms.

Introduction

About the Author

Briefly something about me: My name is Lady Sas. Sas stands for Saskia. I am divorced, live in Frankfurt/Main, and have a grown-up daughter. I have been involved in BDSM for many years. Maybe you have already come across my Femdom blog while browsing the internet? I have been running the blog since 2013 and have published well over 100 interviews with professional dominatrixes, private mistresses and slaves from all over the world on my site. On my blog I also share personal thoughts and provide advice to SM devotees. Please have a look. It is accessible for free: Lady-Sas.com

I have never worked as a professional dominatrix, nor am I a classically trained writer. My job in Frankfurt's financial sector has more to do with numbers than with words. Nevertheless, I enjoy writing down my experiences with my slave Toytoy so that I can share them with others. Writing is great fun for me and I have already published numerous books on the subjects of BDSM, Femdom, and cuckolding.

With this book, I would like to pass on my Femdom knowledge in a targeted and structured way. I want to help you develop from a curious woman to a self-confident, sovereign Femdom who acts out her desires in an enjoyable way. My goal is for men not to be ashamed of their submissive tendencies, but to let go and embrace them without inhibition. Believe me: it's worth it! You will enjoy this new world very, very much.

How Did the Femdom Academy Come About?

How did I come up with the idea of starting a BDSM course in the form of a book? In order to answer this question, I have to elaborate a bit. I have had my sub Toytoy since February 2011. We have a pure BDSM relationship, live separately, and only see each other on the weekends. Toytoy is not my partner, but my sub. I know that in a long-term relationship it is necessary for the Femdom to provide variety every now and then. One of my ideas was to invite curious women to my home and show off Toytoy in his slave role. This usually works out great. My visitors become aware of me and Toytoy through my blog or my books, or I get in touch with them through other channels. In any case, this idea works very well. The ladies enjoy watching an experienced Femdom discipline her sub, I enjoy showing off the slave (pride of ownership), and Toytoy gets great pleasure from having to present himself. This practice has also resulted in several beautiful friendships for which I am very grateful.

These demonstrations are mostly one-off meetings, but there are also some women who are curious to learn more. If they don't live too far away, they become regular guests, and attend a kind of SM course with me. As mentioned above, I like to write, therefore I decided to capture the principles of my training course in a book. Voilá!

Contemporary SM Instead of Clichés from the 90s

BDSM is a topic that has changed significantly over the course of the last decades. When private television came along in the 90s, BDSM was still considered to be forbidden, bizarre, and perverted. Camera teams sensationally pounced on anyone who could hold a whip. Clichés of women in boots brutally whipping rich managers in secret back rooms were haunting people's minds. Fortunately, people today are more enlightened. We are aware that BDSM is not a perversion but should be considered a sexual kink. One does not have to like *50 Shades of Grey*, but it has freed the world of BDSM from its grubby image and made it socially acceptable. Today one can talk about BDSM without blushing. That is beautiful and in keeping with the times. My book aims to portray BDSM as open, modern, and enlightened.

Fortunately, the view has prevailed that BDSM is based on trust, curiosity, and imagination instead of brutal violence. The sub surrenders to the Femdom, trusts her, and submits in an enjoyable role play. In doing so, he makes it possible to imagine a world in which fantasy reigns. What could be more beautiful than two people sharing this world? BDSM is multi-faceted and offers countless possibilities for living out once secret desires and fantasies. In this way, BDSM can enrich one's love life permanently by providing a breath of fresh air. However, there is not only a wide range of possibilities, but also different degrees of intensity with which one can pursue these possibilities. From light to extreme. As you will see, it is not likely to get boring.

Everyone Has to Find Their Own SM Style

I would like to emphasise that there are no laws or rules that clearly regulate BDSM. I am not an authority nor I am so presumptuous as to claim that only I can determine what is right and what is wrong. I can't do that and I won't. Instead, I would like to present my view on the subject and invite every reader to make up his or her own mind. I think, everyone has to individually create their own BDSM style. I am here to help with everyone finding their own way. Instead of prescriptions I offer possibilities, perspectives, and my own experiences. In other words: Do not mistake what I write in this book as law, but as an account of my personal views. Create your own world on this basis. I wish you have a lot of fun doing so.

Lesson 1.

The Mindset of a Femdom and a Sub.

What makes a Femdom? Is it the boots? Or the whip? Handcuffs perhaps? No, these are all just clichés. What makes a Femdom is her mindset. Her mind is her most important asset. **If the mindset is right, everything else comes naturally.** It might sound simple, but unfortunately it is not. Before you can embrace the role a confident, proud Mistress, you first have to shed your insecurities. I think it's natural to have insecurities. I myself was super-insecure at the beginning! And I know from my public display sessions with my sub Toytoy that 80% of all beginners are insecure. So, it's all quite normal and perfectly fine.

Where does this uncertainty come from? I think it results from the following:

1. Many beginners (but also experienced women) know too little about BDSM. They consider their existing knowledge to be insufficient.

2. They have no or little practical experience and don't want to make a mistake.

3. They have not yet accepted their role as a Femdom.

4. They are afraid of not living up to the expectations of their play partner.

Understanding and Living the Role of a Femdom

The first step in shedding these insecurities is to be clear about what role you take on as a Femdom. Being a Femdom - what does that actually mean?

In my understanding, it means taking control and providing leadership. You are now the decision-maker. You are the director. You call the shots. In short, **being a Femdom means leading.** You lead, the sub follows.

This is a new experience for many women. We are used to avoiding conflict and live in harmony with our environment. Suddenly issuing orders and giving direction is alien to us. But we have to get used to it. Harmony, respect, and jointly made decisions are suddenly replaced by an almost dictatorial, egotistic attitude. Yikes, that's pretty unkind, isn't it? Absolutely! But please don't forget: BDSM is just a role play among adults. It is necessary to fill and accept the role of the Femdom, because the sub expects this behaviour. He needs clear instructions. Any insecurity and hesitation on your side will only confuse and unsettle him.

As a Femdom, you don't say, "Excuse me, dear slave, would you mind standing at the St. Andrew's cross now, please?" No, you simply command, "Slave, stand at the St. Andrew's cross!"

You do not say: "Dear slave, would you please be so kind as to fetch me the riding crop?" Rather, you say, "Slave, fetch me the crop."

Give simple, clear commands! And please avoid using "please". If you say "please," it is not a command, but a request. **But slaves expect to hear orders.** They long to obey your orders. Very much so. In a moment I will explain why. First, a word about intonation, i.e. the way you should address the slave.

The Intonation of a Femdom

Insecure Mistresses are often loud, unfriendly, and aggressive. Such women pretend to be particularly merciless and strict, but in reality, they are afraid of making a mistake and try to cover up their insecurities. This type of intonation is wrong. A self-assured Femdom knows that the sub will do whatever she wants. She has no need to raise her voice. What is the point? The slave is not hard of hearing. If she tells him in a calm and relaxed tone: "Slave, fetch me the crop," then he will do so without any hesitation.

An appropriate tone is therefore characterised by superiority, calmness, and coolness. But: This does not mean that the Mistress should act as if she is sedated. She can also react passionately to the sub's mistakes, scold him loudly, and whip his ass. That works too. I think that it is even beneficial when a Femdom shows that she can switch gears. It is wonderful to react emotionally from time to time and let your temper run free. But this should not become the rule. Mistresses without self-control find it difficult to establish long-term relationships with their subs. Men who are not one beer short of a six pack will not put up with such behaviour for long and quickly look for a new Mistress. In conclusion:

Don't pretend to be someone you are not, stay authentic, and don't confuse dominance with volume and aggression.

Why Does a Man Submit?

This brings us to the question of what a sub is actually looking for in a Mistress? Why does a man voluntarily take on the role of a slave? Isn't that stupid? Submitting himself? Why do certain men do that?

Well, their reasons in many ways resemble our own. They want to take time out from boring everyday life. They want to immerse themselves in another world. They want to forget the worries and frustrations of everyday life for a while. They long for an alternative reality that provides them with a possibility to do just that. This alternative reality is called BDSM. The woman slips into the role of the Mistress, the man into the role of the sub.

Taking on the role of a slave is not a sign of weakness, but an expression of inner strength. **We should have respect for it and be grateful that the man engages in this game.** Let us not forget: We are only a Mistress if the man makes us one. If, on the other hand, the man refuses to recognize us as a Mistress, then we can crack the whip as often as we like or stomp our boots angrily - we are not a Mistress, but at best a would-be Femdom. **Mistress and slave need each other.** He needs us, we need him. It is this give and take that is the foundation of any play.

There are many men who are strong, assertive, proactive, and successful in everyday life who like to submit to a Mistress in their spare time. For them, a session is an opportunity to show their submissive side. As a slave they can be passive, weak, helpless, and dependent. The modern man of today cannot show these weaknesses in everyday life. Men always have to perform at their best. Be it at work, in sports, during leisure time, or in bed. Being constantly under this pressure is extremely exhausting. Men cannot even complain about it, without immediately being considered to be a wimp. BDSM offers them an excellent opportunity to shut off their brain, come to rest, or experience something exciting beyond the mundane everyday life. **BDSM resembles a holiday.** You are somewhere else for a limited time, experience something great, and then return to everyday life safe and sound. In this respect, BDSM - far from being a perversion - is more of an adult game that revolves around sexual fantasies. One positive of this game: Providing variety and a breath of fresh air. There is no reason to be ashamed of it. On the contrary, every man deserves respect for being so open and courageous as to defy social conventions and try something new, live out his fantasies, and start this adventure.

Coincidence? Just as I am writing this passage, I receive an email from Slave U. With his permission, I cite his message because it nicely summarizes what subs are looking for.

"Dear Lady Sas,

I have just read your book 'Slave Training Part 1' and I really liked it.

I am still a beginner when it comes to BDSM. A few times I have been with different dominas. Each time it was a very inspiring event and I feel that I can experience so much in it that is otherwise impossible in everyday life. I am married, have a family. And I still dream of visiting a Mistress again. To be allowed to be a slave. To be trained. Dreams, I know. But they are beautiful.

Your blog, the books I have read so far, are incredibly inspiring. Thank you very much for that. The topic of BDSM is still exciting for me. It makes my heart beat faster. Not a daily routine.

Please keep up the good work. I will read your blog and your books.

Love and humble greetings

U. "

Thank you, dear U., I think we can learn a lot from your email.

The Silence Challenge

I have developed a practical exercise through which an aspiring Femdom can learn to let go of her insecurities. I call it the Silence Challenge. The exercise goes like this: You enter a room with a crop in your hand where a slave is kneeling naked on the floor. Preferably in the basic slave position: kneeling upright, legs slightly apart, hands resting on the thighs with the open palms facing upwards, eyes lowered submissively. Your task is to walk around the slave, look at him, and endure the silence in the room. Silence is not so easy to endure. Some people get nervous when it is quiet, especially when they are in a room with another person. They feel the need to say or do something in order to break this silence.

Walk slowly. No, much more slowly. You should not walk, but stride. Put each foot on the floor deliberately. It is best to put on high heels so that you make a noise. Walk slowly around the slave.

Immerse yourself in the experience. Do you feel the fear, the tension, the uncertainty? Breathe in and out deeply and just allow these feelings. Yes, maybe at some point you don't know what to do. Yes, maybe you suddenly go blank and don't have the slightest idea what to do with this naked man.

Yes, maybe your hands suddenly start shaking and you have to press your hands against your body so that the sub doesn't notice. Yes, that's all okay. None of that is a problem, because the slave is still kneeling there. Tense and attentive.

Breathe deeply. The calmness in the room has a message for you. It says: "*Everything is all right. You decide if it's quiet for one minute. Or two or three or four or ten minutes. Only one person determines that: You! And no matter what you decide: It's all right. The slave has no say and respects your every decision. After all, you are the Mistress. That means: You can't do anything wrong!*"

Beginners always have the feeling that they have to act. *Quick, quick! I have to do something! Heavens, what am I doing now? Quick, quick! But I can't think of anything! Help! Blackout! It's all gone! Quick, quick! What am I going to do?*

That is nonsense. The silence in the Silent Challenge teaches you that you don't have to do anything. You can just walk up and down and look at the slave. This is also good. He respects that and even gets nervous under your gaze.

Feel the calm. Feel how you gradually relax, how you sense that you could endure this calm and inactivity even longer. The slave is obliged to absolute passivity in his role. He is not allowed to speak without permission. He is not allowed to stand up without permission. He is not allowed to do anything without permission. **He is 100% passive.**

On the one hand, this is pleasant because you don't have to expect surprises. On the other hand, it challenges you as a leader. **You lead. You have to lead. Otherwise nothing happens.** That can be exhausting at times. But there is no alternative. Your power is based on the fact that you alone plan and know what will happen. If you start debating with him, you give up power and weaken your position. No slave likes that.

As a Femdom, we must first understand that we are almost infallible in our role. Our mere presence is enough to make the slave nervous and aroused. Look, you slowly walk around the sub and he gets more nervous with every step. He is probably in total awe of your high heels and would like to kiss them. Almost all slaves have a shoe and foot fetish. Savour the feeling of superiority caused by being able to bear the silence. Feel how suddenly all insecurities have disappeared. Now feel how self-confidence spreads through your body. Beautiful, isn't it? Now command the slave to kiss your shoes. "Greet me, slave!" - Perfect, dear junior Mistress! Well done.

The Femdom Mindset

Your mindset, i.e. your inner attitude determines your charisma and your effect on the sub. It is therefore important that you are clear about why you are in your role and what this role means. In the following I have summarised the most important points.

- I slip into the role of the Mistress because it excites me, because it's fun, and because it allows me to escape the grey everyday life for a while.
- I realise that I play only a temporary role. Just as my sub only plays a role. After the game, we let go of our roles and meet again as equals.
- I realise that it takes two to play this game. Without my sub, I would not be able to act as a Mistress.
- I also realise that there are limits to everything. I respect my sub's hard limits and I am aware of my responsibility for him.
- I lead the sub. I decide how we play.
- I am active, he is passive.

- I do not have to do anything. I only have to do one thing: Enjoy myself! (And of course respect the hard limits of the sub).
- I give clear orders to the sub and never ask for anything.
- I expect my orders to be carried out instantly with enthusiasm and dedication.
- I don't have to rush. I can decide at my leisure what I feel like doing next.

From my point of view, these are the basics that you have to understand.

Tip: Read through the individual points regularly to fully internalise them.

The Malesub Mindset

The mindset of a male sub is something we also need to look at in depth. Here are my principles:

- I like to take on the role of a sub because it allows me to escape from everyday life. I can switch off my brain and just let myself go. All the pressures that weigh on me fall off. No deadlines, no decisions, no hassles. I just have to obey and enjoy the feeling of being allowed to relinquish leadership and control.

- I love to worship a woman. It's super sexy when a woman sets the tone and uses me the way she wants at that moment. I don't know what's going to happen next and that is exciting.

- I don't submit because I am a weakling, but because I am mentally strong. I have no problem with completely submitting. I am able to surrender and be myself again afterwards: Self-confident, strong and ready for everyday life.

- I accept that the Mistress has absolute power and control over me.

- I love it when a Femdom plays with my sexuality and with my lust. It gives me a kick.

The SSC Principle

In BDSM, SSC does not stand for the football club SSC Naples, but for the concept "Safe, Sane, Consensual". It is an abbreviation of safe, common sense and consensual. SSC describes the foundation on which all participants play. The power of the Femdom finds its limits here. And that is also reasonable. If both partners commit to the SSC principles, it means:

- that everything is based on safe activities (note: safety is dealt with in detail in a later chapter).

- that all participants must be of sound mind to consent, i.e. not be inebriated due to drug or alcohol use.

- that all practices must be consensual and never against the will of any participant.

There are different opinions on what it means the be "safe". If one of the participants assumes that an activity is possibly unsafe, then it must not be carried out. It doesn't matter whether he or she is

31

right or wrong. It is not about who is and who is wrong. What matters is the mutual agreement that a scene is safe. If this agreement has not been reached, the scene must not be played out. It is as simple as that. SSC is also important so that players can distance themselves from actions that could be punishable (for example, because they happen against a player's will).

The principles of SSC are widespread in BDSM. However, there are also practitioners of BDSM who ask themselves: Why should we not play a game that we both want to play just because it is unsafe and dangerous? That's exactly what is thrilling for us! Such people often follow the RACK principle.

The RACK Principle

RACK means: Risk-aware consensual kink. In other words, both partners are aware that their BDSM play involves risks and they take these risks consciously and consensually. "Kink" in this context stands for bizarre games, therefore it is a broader term than BDSM.

So, what does this mean for you? It means that before you play, you should discuss and define the ground rules of the session. This is usually not a big deal. The sub should inquire whether the Mistress plays according to SSC principles. In 95% of the cases he will receive an affirmative answer. It is important to ask because there is a small minority of Femdoms who refuse to adhere to SSC. These women exist. They are of the opinion that they alone have the right to set the rules that the sub has no say in the matter. Do they offer a safe word to the sub so that he can stop the game? No, only the Mistress decides when the game ends.

My urgent advice: Keep your hands off such Femdoms! As a sub, you shouldn't be deceived by the attractive appearance of a woman and think to yourself: Well, it can't be that bad. It can! To be pushed beyond your physical and psychological limits without being able to stop play is a nightmare. It is always better to ask too much than too little.

Short Theory Section

SM, D/S, B&D, TPE, FLR, 24/7, BDSM, Vanilla. The BDSM community seems to have a special fondness for abbreviations and foreign words. I recently read book on SM that describes these terms in detail on more than 30 pages. To be honest: I couldn't finish it. At most I skimmed it, because I didn't really want to know that much. Nothing against a bit of theory, but let's keep it concise.

BDSM is an umbrella term. It covers the categories of S&M (Sadism & Masochism), D&S (Dominance & Submission) and B&D (Bondage & Discipline).

Strictly speaking, S&M or simply SM refer to sadism and masochism. In common usage, however (and in this book, too, by the way), S&M and BDSM are used almost synonymously.

D&S describes the psychological dynamic of dominance and submission. The Femdom dominates, the man submits.

B&D refers to the practice of bondage. The Femdom subjects the sub by force by tying him up.

Finally, people active in the world of BDSM refer to all people who practise conventional sex as vanilla. The term derives from the fact that the most popular type of ice cream is vanilla. According to this school of thought, all normal people only enjoy vanilla while ignoring many other delicious flavours.

An FLR is a Female Led Relationship, i.e. a relationship where the woman is in charge.

More intense than a FLR is a 24/7 relationship. This means that the two players live in their roles 24 hours a day, 7 days a week (at least mentally). Extreme! And definitely too exhausting for me.

The TPE concept is also extreme. It means that the top determines all areas of the sub's life, even finances and social contacts. Often 24/7 and TPE are used as synonyms, but there is a clear difference: 24/7 puts the emphasis on time, TPE on the intensity of the relationship.

Confused?

Everything a bit complicated?

Don't worry, for everyday use the terms SM, D/S and Vanilla are sufficient.

However, it is important to know the terms for the dominant and the submissive part. These are the dominant terms: Femdom, Mistress, Top, and Dom/Domina. And these are the terms for the submissive part: malesub, sub, slave, and bottom. The term "switch" has a special meaning: a switch is a person who combines both submissive and dominant tendencies and plays both roles as he or she pleases, sometimes as a top, sometimes as a sub.

Lesson 2.

The Relationship Between Mistress and Sub.

Having clarified the mindset of the Mistress and the sub, we now turn to the relationship between Mistress and slave. As already mentioned, there are no fixed rules. Everyone is allowed to design their own version of BDSM themselves. Here is some information for your orientation.

The Classic Dominatrix and Her Client

If you asked a professional dominatrix 20 years ago how she treated her client, the answer would have been clear: there is no intimacy at all. The only thing the slave was allowed to touch was the Mistress's boot with his lips and tongue. The dominatrix was addressed formally, while the sub was called by his first name, further emphasising the power imbalance. The dominatrix was fully dressed while the slave was naked. The dominatrix had unconditional authority. Pure and simple. Anyone who did not follow her orders would be punished.

The Bizarre Lady and Her Client

This situation has changed in recent years. Today there are professionals who call themselves "Bizarre Ladies" and who probably outnumber classic dominatrixes by now. Bizarre ladies blur the boundaries between eroticism, fetishism, and sadomasochism. Intimacies are allowed - something completely unthinkable for a classic dominatrix. For example, some of these ladies for offer training for so-called "licking slaves". Bizarre ladies are dominant but more playful than dominatrixes. They don't always insist on being addressed formally, flaunt their assets and don't take the formalities of BDSM so seriously.

What was once completely out of the question is now possible and normal. I am in no position to judge and only give a factual account of the current situation. Every bizarre lady is different. What one enjoys and offers as a service may be completely out of the question for another.

The Femdom and Her Sub Today

Femdoms should ask themselves: What do I want? What turns me on? What feels good? And what would I rather not do? - Those who can answer these questions know how they want to live out their desires and should do just that. The idea that you cannot be a good Mistress if you have sex with your sub is outdated. **Permissible is what likes!** Of course, you can also choose to be an untouchable Mistress and not allow any intimacy, i.e. to follow the style of the classic dominatrix. Anything goes as long as you feel comfortable.

Especially couples who want to try S&M in order to reignite do not want to give up sex. However, I recommend that you do not completely abandon your roles here either and let always the woman decide in which positions and when to get down to business.

A Femdom should not only think of her own desires. **It is important to compare one's own inclinations with those of the sub and to find mutual interests.** But this process of negotiation should never be done explicitly. It is advantageous to keep the sub in the dark about your intentions. He should never know what the Mistress is up to. The best thing is to act as if you are only following your own desires. The sub doesn't need to know how much you are actually catering to his interests.

Rules Help to Distinguish Between Everyday Life and BDSM

In reality, many difficulties occur once the man suddenly has to submit to his wife. I deliberately write "has to" because that is, after all, the basic principle of all female led BDSM. The Mistress leads, the slave follows. Men have no problem with going to a dominatrix as a customer. After all, they don't know the lady from their everyday life. It is easy for them to submit to a beautiful stranger. They love it.

But in a partnership, it is something completely different. Here the man is used to taking the lead or at least being equal to his wife. The fear of no longer being respected by the woman once he has submitted to her as a sub is great. This fear must be taken very seriously. Ignoring it is a mistake.

What to do? My suggestion: Write down some rules of the game. Put it in writing that you are both playing an adult role play. This will reinforce the idea that you are really just slipping into roles, but that you are only playing these roles and not really identify with them. This is important. Your set of rules could look like this, for example:

Rules of the game between Susi and Frank.

- *We engage in an adult role-playing game.*

- *We play our roles, but we do not identify with them.*

- *Susi slips into the role of the dominant, bossy, arrogant, and unapproachable Lady Valetta.*

- *Frank plays the role of the submissive slave 32, who is totally devoted to Lady Valetta.*

- *The session begins as soon as Lady Valetta has put the collar on her slave 32.*

- *The session ends as soon as she has taken the collar off him.*

- *We both commit to staying in our roles during the session.*

- *If one of us no longer wants to continue, he or she says the word "Exit" (safeword). The other one then has to stop immediately under all circumstances.*

- *After the session we are Susi and Frank again.*

- *The aim of the game is having fun.*

Susi and Frank are on the right path. I can recommend all 10 points. It is particularly helpful to give oneself a different name, as in the example here: "Lady Valetta" and "Slave 32". New names are useful from a psychological point of view, because they reinforce the impression that one is immersed in a role but does not identify with that role completely. On the one hand, the name change makes it easier to get into your character. And on the other hand, it is easier to give it up.

It is also helpful to define precisely when the game begins and when it ends. You take on a different character at one exact moment in time and reverse to your real self at another. It is especially important for the sub to find himself on equal terms again once the session is over. Now he has time to process that it was just a game between adults. It is important for the wife to communicate that she doesn't think any less of her husband. Rituals can help to find one's way back into the real world. Even a simple but intimate hug at the end of the session can create this feeling. It can also help to sit down together for a few minutes after the session and discuss it. What was beautiful? What was particularly fun? What should be different next time? Praise each other, emphasise the positives, but also talk openly about difficulties.

Create Your Own Role

Feel free to embellish your role. What qualities does "Lady Valetta" have? What is her background? What moves her, what does she want, what does she want to prevent at all costs? Let off steam, let your imagination run wild. Anything is possible in role play. You can even change your age. Maybe Susi is 54 and Lady Valetta is only 34? Why not? Anything goes.

Example:

Lady Valetta comes from an old Prussian nobility and is incredibly rich. She is interested in theatre and likes to ride horses. She also likes to flirt with the stable boys whom she hires herself. Rumour has it that she occasionally takes one of the young lads to bed with her. But of course these are just rumours.

Her personal slave 32 has been devoted to her for many years. She is dominant, bossy, arrogant, and unapproachable towards her slave. The sub can try as hard as he likes, the fine lady is never satisfied. She constantly finds fault with his work. No wonder she regularly gives the sub a scolding lecture and a spanking to make her point.

When you define your role, take time to choose a **good name**. Don't choose just any name at random. Pick a name that expresses your individual philosophy. A formal title can be very advantageous. Femdoms traditionally have a title that makes them special and exclusive. The following variations of my name can serve as an example:

- Lady Sas

- Mistress Sas

- Mistress Sas

- Madame Sas

- Queen Sas

- Princess Sas

- Baroness of Sas

- Duchess Sas

- Miss Sas

You are now asking yourself what do I mean by "philosophy"? An example will explain. The professional dominatrix Lady Pascal chose her name not randomly but because it refers to the physical unit of pressure: "Pascal". I think, I do not need to explain pressure any further in the context of BDSM.

I also find the German name "Baroness von Stiefelreich" (Stiefelreich = Boot Kingdom) beautiful, because it indicates a special preference for boots. I have conducted numerous interviews with Femdoms for my Femdom Blog and I have always been fascinated by the motivations for particular name choices. Here is a small selection for inspiration.

Lady Sas: How did you come up with your name? Does it have something to do with Tease & Denial? What is the background of your academic title Professor?

Prof. Cara von Teese: The name Professor Cara von Teese has less to do with Tease & Denial. It is rather a combination of my academic family background with my love for the burlesque dancer Dita von Teese. Furthermore, the title Professor adds a small individual component to my persona to distinguish myself from all the 'ladies' and 'misses', at least by name.

Lady Sas: Is there a particular reason why you call yourself "Helen Bates"? Often the name describes a certain attitude or philosophy.

47

Dominatrix Helen Bates: (Laughs) Helen Schneider. The lady was a singer in the 70s/80s and always wore black leather clothes. I saw her on TV as a young girl and I guess that's where my leather fetish comes from ;-) Since I like to play mind games, Bates seemed very fitting as a surname - Helen Bates.

Lady Sas: Do you associate a certain philosophy with your name "Daemona de Lucca"? Is the name supposed to express something specific?

Daemona de Lucca: My roots lie in the gothic scene, where people liked to adorn themselves with "diabolical" names. Those who associate the name with the devil or evil in general are on the wrong track. The guardian spirits (gargoyles) carved on some churches and cathedrals in all four directions symbolise demonic creatures to ward off evil spirits. They say: "Here we are already, get lost!". In a figurative sense, this also fits BDSM. In the end, the strict, evil Mistress is only concerned with her play partner's well-being.

Lady Sas: Dear Madame Curie... no, wait a minute, that's the famous physicist and chemist. Is this association intentional? What is it about your name?

Madame Curie: In my civil life I am a process engineer, so in a broader sense I am a scientist just like Marie Curie. I also love exploring things and pushing boundaries. Both in the field of scientific research and on a human level. I want to find out what drives me and my counterpart (or should I say my sub?) if it's not me and my crop.

Lady Sas: What is the meaning of your name "Anuskatzz"?

Mistress Anuskatzz: Anuskatzz is actually just a nice and absurd wordplay on the name of my favourite body-part, the anus. Already at a very young age it is a very important organ, giving us satisfaction. Its daily use brings about pleasure and emotions of liberation. It balances and cleanses. One of my favourite activities in BDSM is anal play. Therefore, my name speaks for itself. The Katzz with two Zz is based on my film company Dirty Dreaz. All subjects in the films I produce are allowed to create a stage name ending in Z. Since I am the co-founder of the company, I have two Zz! Besides, I just like the pronunciation of Katzz. There's something very elegant but also superior and dominant about it. Just the way a cat is.

Lady Sas: How did you come up with your name?

Eve Dynamite: I just wanted a name with recognition value not used by anyone else.

You find it too difficult to find an adequate name? No problem, just take a name you like and add "Lady". There doesn't always have to be a philosophy behind it.

With slaves, the choice of name is not much easier. By the way, I use the term "sub" as a synonym for "slave". There are different opinions on this matter. Some friends of mine in the scene are of the opinion that a "slave" is below a "sub". Well, as I said, I do not want to dictate anything to anyone or insist on one particular point of view. In this book I use both terms with a consistent meaning. What is meant is simply a man who submits in role-play.

Some inspirations for slave names:

- Sub Toytoy

- Slave Toytoy

- Servant Toytoy

- Slave 32

- Slave Small Cock

- Slave Small Brains

As you can see, some names are meant to humiliate the sub. But it is also possible to associate a certain philosophy with the name. Think about it.

With the name of my own slave Toytoy I want to express his status as a toy for me. I don't like the term "toyboy" so much, but I like "Toytoy". It has a nice ring to it. Most of the time, though, I just say "slave". That's the easiest.

Lesson 3.

Prepare the Session.

The Location

People involved in BDSM use the term "session" when they mean SM dates. Such sessions can take place at home, in SM rental flats, or even outdoors in the forest. To always stay in the same place is boring in the long run, so it makes sense to use Google in order to find a nicely furnished SM flat for rent nearby.

SM flats offer a variety of equipment such as a St. Andrew's cross or a pulley that beginners are unlikely to have in their living room. You can usually rent such flats for a few hours or days. Domina studios also often offer their rooms for rent. It doesn't cost anything to ask, and Google will certainly provide addresses available in your area.

There is no place better than home for you? No problem, here you go! Close the curtains, pull down the blinds, and enter your personal realm of secret pleasures. I recommend using candles to conjure up a special atmosphere. It is best to place the candles in such a way that no fire can break out and you don't accidentally cause a disaster while striking your sub with the riding crop. If possible, clear out the room as much as possible. There is less to worry about and you can focus your attention on your sub.

Music is very important and helps to create the right atmosphere. Music tastes are different. One person loves classical music, another loves dark spherical sounds, while a third enjoys heavy metal. It is all good. I would argue against the radio though. At a crucial moment the weather report might come on and ruin the atmosphere. Surely you can find something more suitable. I recommend turning up the volume. That way the neighbours won't hear about your little adventure. Deafening music, however, is not recommended. After all, the sub should still hear your commands.

One of the most important ingredients for a successful session is time. Take as much of it as possible. **Pleasure needs time.** This is the only way you can relax and really immerse yourself in the world of BDSM. Turn off your mobile phone and take other precautions to have an uninterrupted session. Remember: you want to clear your head. If you constantly have something in the back of your mind, it will be distracting and you won't be able to enjoy the session. Ideally you start with the preparations the day before so that you can fully concentrate on the SM date.

Instruct the slave to take a fresh shower and wait for you kneeling naked on the floor. Meanwhile you can dress up. Tip: It would be a waste of time, if you get all dressed up and only approach the sub afterwards. It makes much more sense to send him to the bathroom first. This gives the sub time to acclimatize, slip into his role, and get in the right mood for the session.

A point that is often forgotten: Consider whether the temperature in the playroom is okay for the sub. A naked slave should not freeze. But neither should he sweat. Make sure the temperature is right.

What Should I Wear?

Subs have it easy when it comes to choosing clothes. He must present himself stark naked. The only thing a sub is allowed to wear is his collar. Hand and ankle cuffs are also okay. The contrast between the clothed Mistress and the naked slave beautifully expresses the power imbalance. The term for this dynamic is CFNM (Clothed Female Naked Man).

The Mistress can wear whatever she wants. Who do you want to be today? What suits your role? Are you the strict leather dominatrix with high black boots or the elegant lady in a costume with high heels? Or maybe you want to excite the slave with a pair of sexy hot pants?

I don't want to bore you with make-up and styling tips. After all, this is an S&M guide and not a women's magazine or a beauty blog. My advice: Wear something special that makes you feel comfortable and desirable. Almost all subs have a fetish for high heels. Take this into account as much as possible, if you want to do your slave a favour. Personally, I think elegant shoes with pointed, high heels are an absolute must. It is incredible how high heels improve one's posture (and thus also one's inner posture).

You have absolutely no idea what to wear? Try a classic outfit: pencil skirt, black panty hose or stockings, black high-heels, and a white blouse. This way you will definitely be well dressed and come across as confident. I would argue against outfits that are too revealing, showing too much bare skin. But that's a matter of personal taste. There are also women who like to show off their female charms and tantalise the sub's carnal desires.

In preparation for the session, organize your SM instruments in an orderly fashion. It doesn't look very confident if you have to spend a long time looking for your favourite whip during play.

Lesson 4.

Start the Session.

I recommend that you start and end the session with a ritual. As already mentioned, rituals make the transition in and out of the session easier. It is also possible to combine several rituals. An opening ritual can look like this:

The Mistress enters the room with the slave in the basic slave position: He kneels naked with his upper body upright, legs slightly spread, hands resting on his thighs with the open palms facing upwards, gaze lowered submissively. The Mistress slowly walks towards the sub. She stops and examines him. After that she circles him so that she can inspect him from all sides. Finally, she stands in front of the slave again.

Greeting the Mistress

"**Greet me**", the Mistress demands and puts one foot forward. Immediately the slave crawls toward her, bends down low, and kisses her shoe. Most men execute this command far too quickly without the necessary dedication. You almost always have to remind beginners to kiss slowly and intensively. This ritual is about giving the sub the opportunity to submit to the Mistress and worship her. She determines how exactly she wants her shoes to be worshipped. It is common for the sub to slowly and intensively kiss them from all sides. Since his kisses are an expression of his submission and dedication he should not rush but proceed calmly without haste.

Many Mistresses love firm kisses so that they can feel the pressure of the sub's lips through the leather. I also would recommend this, but as I said, individual preferences might differ. You can also have your shoes licked clean. If the sub has been naughty lately or if he is into humiliation, then the Mistress can sit him down and remind him of the great honour to worship her shoes. All he is good for is to lick the soles of her shoes.

Don't make the mistake of moving your feet while the sub worships them. They simply remain in place. The sub has to crawl around them if he wants to kiss the shoe from all sides. This gives an amusing sight from above that you do not want to miss. "Don't forget the heel" is a standard phrase in this exercise.

When you have had enough, pull one foot back and put the other forward.

Say, "Now the other one."

Or: "I have two feet, slave."

Get into the habit of giving orders verbally. In their role, subs are condemned to passivity. They are not even allowed to say a peep without being asked. So, it is up to you to talk. A woman who does not speak during the session misses the chance to turn a decent session into a very good session. I will come back to this in a later chapter. For now, I would like to give you the advice: **Talk! It makes the session infinitely better. Play with the sub's imagination and practice your verbal skills.** We'll see exactly how.

Back to the ritual. After the proper greeting it is time to put the collar around his neck. Or you can order him to further engage with your shoes by having him "blow" your heels, i.e. suck them as if it were a dildo. That's it! Your session has begun.

Let's summarise: Rituals help us to start the session and find our role. In principle, the beginning of a session can be quite simple.

- The slave kneels in the basic slave position.

- The Mistress examines him.

- The Mistress gives the order to greet her and puts one foot forward.

- The sub worships the Mistress's high heels.

- The Mistress collars the sub.

- The session can start.

Practical Tips

Dear Mistress, please join me for a short exercise. It will only take a few minutes. Please assume the slave position I described above. Kneel on the floor with your upper body upright, legs slightly apart, hands resting on your thighs with the open palms facing upwards, eyes lowered submissively. Beautiful. Now try to hold this position for 5 minutes.

Quite strenuous, isn't it? This exercise is intended to show you that waiting a long time for your Mistress in a kneeling position is no walk in the park. **A good Femdom puts herself in her sub's shoes and can draw valuable conclusions from this.** If you order your sub to wait for you in the basic slave position and take around 20 minutes to change into your outfit, then you can almost certainly assume that he will not remain in this position. After all, there is no one there to check. An average sub will kneel down for a minute, then realise "Oh, this is really tiring, I should really do more exercise" and lazily sit on his bum. He will wait for the clacking of your high heels and by the time you enter the room, quickly switch back to the required position, pretending that he knelt obediently all the time. Feel free to ask him if he has been waiting for you like this. Most slaves will not admit to have cheated. But you know better and now you already have a first reason to punish the sub. The slave will be surprised that you have caught him. Your explanation is simple: "The Mistress knows everything." And, "I know you!" A little knowledge of human nature is all that it takes to control and impress subs over and over again.

As a matter of principle, I recommend testing new practices on yourself before trying them out on the sub. This also includes all implements like whips, floggers, clamps, etc. In the past, there were SM studios where the dominatrix first had to serve as a slave herself for a short time so that she could experience first-hand what it's like to be a sub. Today this process has largely been forgotten. But it still makes sense.

Practical Examples

- There are ways you can make the wait period more entertaining for the sub. For example, you can ask a shoe fetishist to polish a pair of boots with his tongue.

- You can also lock the sub in a dark room, additionally blindfold him, fix his hands behind his back, and instruct him to sort some pairs of shoes. Of course, you have to thoroughly mix them up before to make the sorting worthwhile.

- Another suggestion: You order the sub to get on all fours and place a pair of high heels on his back. In this position he must now wait for you. This is not easy, but doable if you have yourself somewhat under control. In my opinion, it is clearly easier than waiting in the basic slave position. There are many nice ways to use the time you need to get dressed for the session. The sub can merge into his role during this time.

Always keep the sub guessing about what will happen next. This stimulates his imagination. Telling him directly what you have in mind for him is a mistake. It ruins the excitement and is comparable to letting the air out of a nice colourful balloon. Who enjoys unwrapping a present when they already know what's inside? It is better to just give hints and thus stimulate his curiosity and imagination.

A Mistress Does Not Need a Reason

I just mentioned that you already have a reason to punish the sub if he lies to you about having lasted 20 minutes in the basic slave position (this is extremely unlikely). This implies that the Mistress needs a reason to punish. But she doesn't. She can also punish the slave without any reason. Just like that. Simply because she wants to. Under no circumstances get involved in a discussion with the sub. You might hear: But Mistress, I haven't done anything wrong, so you mustn't punish me. Or: But, Mistress, I didn't do it on purpose! Please, don't punish me. You must immediately and forcefully end such pleading. **A Mistress does have to not explain herself. She decides and leads.** A slave who does not respect this will be punished. Immediately. You *must* even punish him. If you don't, you will lose your authority. Please remember: You do not have to justify anything. You are not accountable to the slave. You do what you want. It is as simple as that. Why? Because you are a Mistress and not a mouse who first has to ask the master slave for his opinion.

There are slaves who want to test the Mistress. Most of the time, these are men are still beginners as submissives. Or men who just want to try BDSM for fun. They challenge the Mistress by clearly and deliberately breaking the rules. If she lets the slave get away with this kind of disobedience she immediately loses authority. The only option is to take immediate action and punish the misbehaviour without pardon. Otherwise, she risks having the reins taken out of her hands. A common infringement of unruly subs consists in not properly addressing the Mistress. Others include touching the Mistress, speaking without permission, being demanding, or ignoring an order from the Mistress.

In all of these cases, the punishment must be swift and certain. The more severe the offence, the more intense the punishment.

Topping from the Bottom

Topping from the bottom is also not an uncommon behaviour among subs. The sub tries to influence the session from his subordinate position by demanding to be treated in a certain way. Such subs are called "wish list slaves". If you catch your sub behaving in this way, talk to him openly about it. Ask him if he considers himself to be a "wish list slaves," and whether he wants to impose his wishes on you. Usually slaves react meekly when you call out their behaviour as topping from the bottom. Do not get involved in arguments. Listen calmly to the slave's suggestions, but don't let him get away with all of it and always decide for yourself in the end. Remember: BDSM is a game that should be fun for both of you. But: Don't do anything you don't like.

A sure way of getting the slave out of the habit of topping from the bottom is refusing to fulfil his wishes. He talks about facesitting? Then don't do it. He fantasises about a specific pair of high boots he would like to see on you? Then punish him by not wearing them. Tell him in no uncertain terms that you're foregoing them today because you won't let yourself be dominated by a sub and that you don't respond to "wish list slaves" as a matter of principle. Topping from the bottom? Not with you!

It's not what you say, but how you say it. It is perfectly fine for a sub to politely express his dreams, wishes, and desires before the session. But if he makes demands or tries to pressure you, then he is a "wish list slave" and should receive the appropriate stern response. Being amenable to politely expressed wishes of the sub is acceptable as long as they coincide with your own preferences. But I would punish a demanding attitude by not doing what the sub wants from me.

Lesson 5.

The Language of a Mistress.

How does a Femdom talk to her sub? We have already touched on this topic, but in this chapter, we want to take a closer look. Sure: A Mistress doesn't ask - she orders. And she does so with a clear and confident voice. **After all, it's not only what you say that matters. It's also how you say it.**

Practice Exercise

Try this out right now. Stand up, straighten up as much as possible, put both hands on your hips, and say with a loud, clear, and distinct voice: "Greet me, slave!"

That's it. Now put your hands behind your back, look down at the floor and murmur, "Greet me, slave."

Ah, yes, that doesn't feel so exciting, does it? Your posture and voice must express self-confidence and communicate your inner attitude. Realise: You are not just anyone, you are the Mistress. This is your show. You alone determine what happens. Behave accordingly.

Role Models are Not Always Easy to Find

You have probably already browsed the internet for Femdom videos in order to learn something from experienced ladies. In principle, this is a good idea although it comes with some caveats. Unfortunately, there are many women out there who play the role of a dominatrix without any knowledge of BDSM.

On the one hand, there are women who are very pretty but are only capable of dishing out extremely brutal (!) beatings. Obviously, the video director put a cane in the hand of a 20-year-old model and said: "Hit the slave as hard as you can." This is totally out of line! Please don't watch these videos since they convey a false sense of what BDSM is all about. Extreme brutality leads nowhere. It's only attractive for pain fetishists. Leave it alone.

Then there are women who look great but have no idea and no concept of what a Mistress actually does. Here, young models are put in front of the camera and being told: "Okay, we have no script and no idea what we want to shoot. Just improvise something and look good doing it!" The model has no idea either and sits down to light a cigarette. "Lick my boots, slave," she says. Yes - and that was it. The slave licks the boots, the Mistress smokes. Otherwise she says nothing. Could it be any more boring? I don't think so.

Conclusion: Not every video in which a woman appears as a dominatrix is suitable. Some performers simply know nothing about the subject and lack any imagination. Taking them as a role model would lead you astray. Depictions of authentic and realistic BDSM are hard to find.

Now that I have pointed out what is difficult you might ask for positive examples. I have a hard time giving recommendations, because I hardly know any. The professional dominatrix Lady Cheyenne de Muriel from Stuttgart produces videos I enjoy. Just to clarify, I interviewed her once for my blog, otherwise I have no contact with her and receive no commission for my recommendation. What I particularly like about Lady Cheyenne are her stimulating verbal communication skills. This is called "verbal eroticism" or "dirty talk". I also try to talk a lot during my sessions and thus stimulate my sub's imagination. If you are silent all the time, then you miss a big chance. For the slave, the session is at least twice as stimulating if it includes verbal eroticism. You can learn more about verbal eroticism in my autobiographical books. In

Suddenly a Dominatrix, 48 Hours of BDSM, Slave Exchange, and *Domina Duel* I try to portray authentic S&M.

The Art of Verbal Eroticism

In my opinion, the extremely powerful art of verbal eroticism is completely underestimated. A Mistress can use words to create scenes in the sub's mind that push him towards his limits. These scenes would go too far if the Mistress would enact them, but they inspire the slave's erotic imagination. You can think of anything, but you should not act it out. Effective verbal eroticism is based on the ability to negotiate between "I could never do that" and "This is a sexy experience". **The slave experiences a scene in his mind but not in reality.** This is verbal eroticism. It makes any session much more intense.

Example:

Many subs find the idea of being forced by their Mistress to prostitute themselves and service cocks arousing. They revel in the fantasy, but they would never, ever do it in real life. The Mistress's verbal skills can help them to live out this scenario in their imagination. After she put on a strap-on – an artificial cock fitted into a harness - the slave has to kneel in front of the Mistress and suck it. By the way: Any Mistress who understands the intricacies of verbal eroticism will always speak of the strap-on as her "cock". That is much more exciting in the slave's mind. In order to spur on the slave, she could talk in the following way:

"Kneel down, slave. Go on, suck my cock! As a good TV whore, you must be able to suck well when I send you to the whorehouse. Yeah, dive into it! Yeah, that's it. And no teeth! Use your lips and tongue. You're gonna have to do better than that, little blow whore. Come on! Don't pretend you don't like it. Try harder! The gentlemen on the street demand first-class service. You don't want to embarrass your Mistress, do you?"

Another Example:

The Mistress has locked the slave's penis in a chastity belt. Chastity is a highly exciting topic, we will talk about in detail later. The term chastity belt is somewhat misleading, since it has nothing to do with a belt. Chastity cage is more precise. The device is fastened to the penis and testicles and locked with a small metal lock. A common abbreviation for the device in German is KG (chastity belt). Chastity as a practice in the BDSM community is based on the prolonged denial of the sub's orgasm. He cannot masturbate nor pleasure himself in any other way growing more and more frustrated. Most slaves have no experience with a chastity device and already encounter problems after wearing them for only a few hours. And practical concerns oftentimes interfere with chastity training. **But in her imagination the Mistress can exaggerate.** Like this:

"There, slave. Now your cock is mine. Only I can free you from your little prison now. But who knows... maybe I don't feel like it? Why should I unlock you? Such a small mini dick is useless for anything. It's an insult to every woman. It's ridiculous. No, a mini dick like that should be locked away. Maybe I won't even let you out of the cock cage... Maybe I'll keep you chaste from now on and only release you once a month. Or... only once a year. For your birthday or something. Yes, that would be a really good idea. Wouldn't it, slave?"

Reality plays no role in verbal eroticism. It is simply cancelled. In the example above, the actual size of the sub's penis does not matter. Even well-endowed subs can be mocked and ridiculed for being insufficient. Usually, this form of verbal humiliation is called "small penis humiliation", i.e. humiliation based on a supposedly small dick. Many subs love this type of degradation. The example also ignores the fact that most chastity devices are anything but escape-proof. And of course, it would be very extreme to let a man climax only once a year. But in your imagination, anything goes. And yes, it can be very appealing to mentally explore these extreme fantasies.

A Third Example:

A slave who has a penchant for humiliation and high heels might hear the following from his Mistress:

"I am actually much too soft with you, slave. I should walk through the city in my heels and never miss a puddle. I should step in every pile of dirt. Yeah, that's it. And then you can lick all the dirt off my heels. And don't you dare leave a single speck of dust behind, slave! Then I'll kick your ass! And you'll get a beating like you've never experienced before."

Many women find it difficult to use verbal eroticism to arouse a man. For them, this kind of language is too dirty. "Ass pussy"? "I'll fuck you senseless"? "Little cocksucker?" Oh my! That is not very refined, is it? Feel free to use a more restrained language. As always, I'm only giving you suggestions and pointing out possibilities. But remember: Most men are attracted to rather harsh language. It turns them on. **They love it when they hear dirty words from a Ladies mouth. It is unfamiliar and therefore all the more appealing.** My experience: The more explicit the language, the more aroused the sub. But: I also draw boundaries. For me, gutter language has no place in a session.

Don't complain about being the sole entertainer. It is your role to direct the scene. You must raise the intensity level of the situation through targeted verbal eroticism. I deliberately use the word "must" and not "should". In my eyes, it is really your job as a Mistress to use verbal eroticism. If you refuse to engage in this type of play you waste the enormous potential of language and a less intense session is the result.

Don't worry, you don't have to be a master of verbal eroticism right away. Practice as much as possible. Observe the sub, pay attention to his reactions, and experiment a bit with his imagination. What triggers a strong reaction in him? How can you use words to present him with a vivid image that will arouse him? What a nice task! You will eventually realise that there is great power in the art of verbal eroticism. After a while you will know exactly which words arouse your sub and turn him into the most obedient slave possible.

Lesson 6.

One Session and 1,000 Possibilities.

How does the session continue? What will happen next? Every Femdom has her own way of conducting a session. Some are of the opinion that you should not plan anything at all, but act out of the spur of the moment. Just let yourself drift, be spontaneous, and follow your feelings. On the other hand, there are Mistresses who meticulously prepare a session and think long and hard about what they want to do. I can understand if beginners want to grapple with their insecurities by making an exact plan in advance. But I won't recommend it. Instead of liberating your desires, it only cements the insecurity even more.

It is better to think about the general direction of the session for a few minutes at the most, so that you can prepare the appropriate utensils. The central question is: **What do _I want to do_?**

Of course, SM is a give and take. It makes sense and is advisable to respond to the inclinations and wishes of the sub. But avoid doing only what you think the slave might like. It will only frustrate you and sooner or later you will hang up the whip. By acting this way, you don't help anyone. It is better to focus on your own inclinations and only consider the sub's wishes when it meshes with your own plans. You will see: It feels much, much better. The sub will notice your pleasure as well. **He will feel how much pleasure the session gives you.** Many subs derive great satisfaction from the fact that their Mistress enjoys their training. This knowledge is a great turn-on for them. In the end, your supposedly selfish attitude benefits both you and your sub.

Conclusion: Feel free to be selfish. But also try to take the sub's wishes into account in the session as much as possible.

Don't make the mistake of trying to fit 1,000 ideas into one session. It will go wrong. Instead, it is better to focus on two or three practices that you really feel like doing. The world of BDSM is as wide as the ocean. There is an infinite amount of practices to discover and try out. In the following, I will introduce you to the most important practices. Decide for yourself whether this appeals to you or not. Just pick out what turns you on. You can bracket everything else.

The Most Important S&M Practices

Anal Play

Anal play is extremely popular with both Femdoms and malesubs. One also speaks of "pegging". Here a perfect role reversal takes place. Instead of the man penetrating the woman, it is she who fucks his ass. This reversal of the traditional relationship between male and female is very appealing because one can experience something completely new and different. The Mistress feels an intense power rush that is often described as an "orgasm in the head". The slave surrenders and often experiences pegging as humiliating, which exerts a strong sexual attraction. In this respect, it is hardly surprising that pegging is a very common practice in the BDSM community.

Which position is best for anal play? Very popular is the position where the slave lies with his belly over a rack, a spanking bench, or over a stable table. His legs are spread, his buttocks sticking out. Often, he is fixed to the rack with hand and foot cuffs so that he cannot fight back. But this is only one element to stimulate his imagination. Of course, everything happens consensually and never against the sub's will.

The Mistress stands behind the sub and approaches him with her strap-on. This is a much more comfortable position for the Mistress than, for example, the riding position. The sub is completely at her mercy. She can see him, but he cannot see her. Another useful side effect: While standing, the Mistress also has optimal control over her strap-on.

The missionary position is rather unusual for pegging. On the one hand, because it is physically strenuous for the Mistress and, on the other hand, because she can use the strap-on with more precision while standing up. I would like to emphasise that there is no right or wrong way when it comes to positions. If it feels right, do it! The position on the rack has practical advantages. But if you prefer to have fun in a different position - go ahead, enjoy! In the end, you shouldn't listen to what others say, but do what you feel most comfortable with.

Especially subs who have little or no experience with strap-on cocks must be introduced to this practice gently. Slaves can relax better if they know they are in good hands and the Mistress knows what she is doing. Confidence in the Femdom is the best remedy against fear. **A woman who is not that**

experienced can still build confidence by going slowly and gently. I recommend using disposable gloves to slowly stretch the sub's anus and also use plenty of lube. The sub then notices that he is dealing with a sensitive Mistress and starts to relax.

Tip: Before you do anything at all, massage the sub tenderly and with both hands until he has adjusted to the situation. Gently run your hands over his back, buttocks, and legs. Take away his fear by assuring him that he will like it and that you will be gentle with him. Feel free to use the power of verbal eroticism. Use phrases like "I'm going to ride you in nice and gently, little mare", "your ass pussy is mine" or something along those lines.

When the slave is ready to let himself go, slip on disposable gloves and put plenty of lube on the index or middle finger. Tell the sub that you now want to test how tight he is and whether he is already broken in. Now very gently, slowly, and carefully insert your finger into the sub's anus. Be careful not to hurt him. Take your time and talk reassuringly to the sub. **He must relax and open up, then it won't hurt.** Slowly slide your finger

83

back and forth until a fucking motion occurs. Tell the sub what you are doing. "Yes, that's it, slave. Now I'm going to fuck your tight little ass pussy!" If the movements do not meet any resistance, try inserting a second finger - and then a third. If the anus is too tight for three fingers, then leave it at two (one is also okay). Every slave is different. One can take incredibly large dildos, the other already whines with only one finger in his butt. Take his moaning and other reactions seriously. Rather be too soft than too hard. You have the responsibility for the sub's health and the anal region is very sensitive. Use plenty of lube and never get carried away. You are endangering the sub with fast or jerky movements. Anal play is fun but it is also not without risk. Be sure to proceed slowly and gently. Then everything should go well. Pay attention to the sub's reactions. Ask him if everything is all right. If the sub feels pain that is unpleasant, you should stop. Pain causing pleasure is okay, but do not ignore a screaming, moaning sub.

Once the sub is well stretched, you can gently insert the strap-on cock - wearing a condom, of course. Make sure that its width is not overwhelming for him. You must not force the strap-on into the anus. Be sensitive and pay attention to the sub's reactions. Is his moaning a sign of pleasure or pain? If the reaction does not seem pleasurable, pull back and ask the sub what is going on. Perhaps you haven't applied enough lubricant? Or the sub is tense and afraid? Or the strap-on is too big? Take your time to find out what the problem is. Don't put yourself under pressure too much pressure and don't be in a hurry. If it doesn't work now, maybe it will next time. Take away the sub's fear. Even if he claims not to be afraid: Beginners almost always have a bit of jitters.

If everything goes smoothly, the strap-on slides into the anus. Comment on what you are doing. You can also place the sub in front of a mirror, then he will be able to see what you are doing. Slowly increase the tempo, grab the sub by the hips, and let your passion run free. Enjoy the feeling of power and fuck the slave properly. Slap him hard on the buttocks from time to time and make sure to tell him know what a great honour it is to be taken by his Mistress.

Now a few words about the shape of the strap-on. The most important features are comfort and pleasure. Anything that hurts is not acceptable. For beginners, thin and short dildos are okay. Especially early on, it's all about reducing the slave's fear and helping him to enjoy the role reversal. A man who was once overwhelmed by a huge dildo will hardly want to experience anal play again.

The size of the strap-on, by the way, is often completely misjudged. **Pegging is not about size, nor about stimulating the butt. It is about stimulating a completely different part of the body: the brain.** The hottest thing about anal play is the idea of doing something "forbidden," something exciting, extreme, taboo. This psychological dimension represents the greatest attraction of anal play. A good Mistress knows this and therefore verbally stimulates the slave. This stimulation is much more exciting for him than the biggest strap-on. It is not about the equipment but about sending the sub on a journey of complete submission. He wants to let go, experience something new, get to know a new role, and be sexually stimulated.

A Mistress who just silently penetrates her slave

has understood nothing. She squanders about 90% of the potential of anal play.

The position I have described above is well suited for beginners as well as for advanced practitioners. The slave can assume a relaxed position and the Mistress has optimal access to his anus. I also recommend a love swing, with the slave in a reclined position and his legs spread apart. If you play in a well-equipped SM studio or SM flat, you should also think about using the gynaecological chair.

Cosmopolitan magazine once interviewed me as a "pegging expert" and asked, "Do you think more men should try pegging?"

My answer: "No, I wouldn't say that. I think it's good if someone is open to new experiences, but every man should decide for himself if that's something for him or not."

For most Femdoms, playing with a strap-on is extremely appealing. But if the sub doesn't feel like it, then you shouldn't do it. Such a practice should never be forced.

Tip: You can prepare the sub for your strap-on by inserting an anal plug at the beginning of the session. This will stretch the anus over time.

Tip: In the pharmacy, the sub can purchase an enema. A liquid is introduced into the colon to clean it out. This way the sub is well prepared for his anal training.

I would also like to mention "fisting". Fisting is the practice of inserting an entire hand into the anus. This is clearly not for beginners. It is best to proceed slowly when it comes to anal stretching.

10 golden rules for anal pleasure.

1. Proceed slowly and carefully. You should avoid hectic movements at all costs. Never pull anything out of the anus quickly.

2. Use plenty of lubricant.

3. Spur on the sub's imagination with verbal eroticism.

4. Latex gloves are best (thin, very stretchy material).

5. Use silicone-based or very thick water-soluble lubricant. (Grease-based agents degrade rubber. Vaseline breaks down gloves and condoms).

6. When you gently press your fingertip into the anus, you will usually feel a reflexive contraction. This is normal, just hold your finger still until the sub relaxes.

7. The golden rule for the sub is: Relax!

8. And the silver rule: Trust the Mistress!

9. And the bronze rule: Communicate! If something hurts, inform the Mistress.

10. Don't force anything. Try it another time.

Cock&Ball Bondage

In BDSM, the term Cock&Ball Bondage refers to the practice of tying up the penis and testicles of the sub. Often, both testicles are separated individually and made to stick out. In this way, the Mistress has the man's "crown jewels" right in front of her so that she can use them for all types of CBT (see Cock-and-Ball-Torture). For CBT, Cock&Ball Bondage is also a safety measure, because it prevents the vas deferens from twisting and the testicles cannot shift into the abdominal cavity.

It is stimulating for the slave to be intimately bound in this way. Because it is important for the blood to continue circulating, the bondage must not be too tight. I recommend using an elastic material for tying. A long nylon stocking is ideal (cut off the lace edge at the top beforehand).

A testicular bondage causes the already sensitive skin of the scrotum to become even more sensitive and thus even more prone to injury. Small, bleeding skin tears occur very easily. Although these are usually harmless, they carry a risk of infection if they are not treated quickly and correctly.

Tip: Knots in nylon stockings are difficult to undo. Take this into account and have a pair of

Lister scissors ready. These are special scissors that can be used to undo bandages.

Tip: There are instructional videos on YouTube. For example, search for "Cock Bondage Tutorial" or "Testicle Bondage".

Human Ashtray

The Mistress uses the sub as an ashtray. Especially at SM parties this is an interesting demonstration of power. The sub kneels next to the Mistress while the she flicks the ashes of her cigarette in his mouth. Of course, this is not particularly healthy, but everyone has to decide for themselves whether to engage in this practice.

Breath Control

This practice is about making the sub directly feel the absolute power of the Mistress. She controls the slave's breathing by, for example, pressing both hands on the sub's nose and mouth. I hope, it is clear to everyone that this practice is dangerous and requires great trust. It is thrilling for the sub to be completely under the control of the Mistress. And the Mistress enjoys the intoxicating feeling of power over the sub. When the slave struggles for breath his body releases adrenaline and endomorphins, intensifying his sexual arousal.

I would like to emphasise that asphyxiation is not to be taken lightly and can be very dangerous. Especially if the sub has a heart condition. Think carefully about whether you want to try this. BDSM offers countless possibilities and you don't have to try out everything just because you can.

An alternative practice is so-called "facesitting". The Mistress sits on the sub's face wearing a pair of vinyl pants, for example, so that he cannot breathe. She lets him wriggle for a few moments - and finally releases him by sliding to the side and letting him breathe again. This practice can also be done with masks. A variant of breath control is to connect a container with the Mistress's to the sub's mask. The sub has to breathe in the scent of the Mistress's urine. Whether this is a reward or a humiliation varies from sub to sub.

Blindfolds

Blindfolds are a double-edged sword. Most subs don't like them because they prefer to admire the fair sex. However, in not using them, you miss out on the experience of what it's like to sharpen the other four senses. Make sure that the blindfold fully restricts the vision of the sub and is not semi-transparent. Otherwise he might be able to cheat. A silk scarf, for example, works well. Or you can get a blindfold from a sex shop. Once the sub is wearing the blindfold, you can start playing with his other senses. Let him feel you - by caressing him tenderly with a flogger. Let him smell you – by having him breathe in your perfume. Let him taste you – by swallowing your spit (see spitting).

Ballbusting

The term ballbusting describes the practice of kicking the sub where it hurts the most: in the balls. A spirited kick in the testicles is the ultimate pain and quickly pushes any slave to his limits. If the Mistress is dealing with a masochistic sub, he will enjoy this extreme pain. For a purely submissive slave, on the other hand, the very idea of getting his balls busted causes fear and horror.

He will therefore do anything to avoid this excruciating pain. Hence, ballbusting can be used as an extremely effective training device. The Mistress can kick with her bare foot until she gets a feel for this practice. Once she gets the knack of it she can start kicking while wearing shoes. Because of its intense effects, I strongly recommend approaching ballbusting slowly and to increase the intensity only cautiously. The testicles are very sensitive and can get injured if the Femdom is not careful. I advise subs interested in ballbusting to only place themselves in the hands of a lady who is responsible and whom they trust.

Bastinado

Bastinado is a type of punishment that involves the caning of the sub's bare feet. Since the sole of the foot contains many nerve endings, this practice is very painful. Advantage: No visible marks remain. Bastinado is mostly administered with a cane, but nothing speaks against using a riding crop, which is less painful.

Punishment

An essential element in S&M. The Mistress punishes the sub for transgressions. His mistakes do not necessarily have to be real, a Mistress always finds reasons for punishment. For many slaves, punishment represents a real fetish. A professional dominatrix told me about a client who regularly visits her to be severely caned. "He simply needs to be beaten. If he doesn't get his spanking, he's simply not balanced," the Mistress explained to me.

However, punishments do not have to be as draconian as in this example. They can also be carried out more gently.

Punishments are an interesting field for psychologists, because the desire to be punished can grow into a real obsession. Perhaps it is a compensation for guilt? I am not a psychologist, but I know that it is important for many slaves to be punished and experience the feeling of relief afterwards. Sometimes they even leave the session euphoric.

Cocksucking

The Femdom shoves her strap-on in his mouth: "Suck my cock!". Any beginner is ready for this task right away. Use a condom and cheer your sub on to do his best. Encourage him to deep-throat your cock. Give him clear instructions and enjoy the show.

Bondage

Bondage refers to use of physical restraints for erotic stimulation. Many subs like being vulnerable and feeling helpless. Men are generally stronger than women. If the slave is tied up, he can no longer use his physical strength and is completely under the control of the Mistress. Giving up power and being in a helpless position represents a strong attraction for the sub.

Many materials can be used for bondage. One of the most common ones is rope. Bondage is a science in itself. The basic rule underlying all forms of bondage is that no nerves or blood vessels are cut off. For those who are interested, I recommend studying a textbook and attending a bondage seminar. These are offered by professional dominatrixes and other BDSM-instructors.

You can also wrap your slave with plastic foil. However, make sure that the sub does not suddenly topple over. The foil completely immobilises him and is unable to catch his fall.

Especially for beginners, it is the easiest for the slave to wear hand and ankle cuffs. These are leather straps that are buckled around the wrists and ankles. Each is attached to a metal ring. The Mistress can use these four metal rings to tie the slave to a St. Andrew's cross, a pulley, or spreader bars. Spreader bars are metal bars that keep the slave's legs apart.

A sub who is into bondage should only play with a Femdom he trusts implicitly. Once you are tied up, you can no longer defend yourself and are at the Mistress's mercy.

Since you probably don't have a basement full of bondage gear and a rack does not look very good in the living room, you can also use everyday household furniture. For example, you can instruct your sub to bend over a sturdy table and then fix him in this position. The sub should wear hand and foot cuffs for this purpose, which you then attach to the table legs with special bondage ropes.

Stable beds are also suitable for restraining the sub. Make sure in advance that the furniture you are using is sufficiently stable.

Tip: Make the slave use the bathroom before you tie him up using intricate knots.

Nettles

Nettles are an excellent means to make masochistic subs suffer. It is ideal for outdoor games in the forest. I will go into more detail on this topic in the section on "Cock and Ball Torture".

Nipple Play

Men's sexuality is mostly fixated on the penis. But cock and balls are only the primary sexual characteristics. Men also have nipples. Playing with them reminds men that stimulating secondary sexual characteristics can also be arousing. The Mistress should proceed with a mixture of reward and punishment (carrot & stick), caressing the nipples tenderly at first and then drilling her fingernails into them, twisting and punching the nipples. There are also special nipples clamps. If you don't want to spend the money, you can also use clothes pegs. One can also use ice cubes, candles, and weights.

But one should not overdo it. A blog reader once described an unpleasant experience to me. He was a client at a very well-known dungeon in Düsseldorf. He emphasised to the young, beautiful dominatrix that she should not leave any marks on his body. The young lady enjoyed torturing his nipples with her fingernails. After the session marks were clearly visible. He complained and was assured that the management of the dungeon would look into the matter. But it did not change the fact that he was left with marks. One should never underestimate how quickly one can inflict or receive marks. We also learn that even renowned and well-known dungeons do not always treat their clients correctly.

Nipple clamps can cause bruising or even damage the tissue if they are too tight and applied for too long. A few minutes should be fine, though. Pay attention to the sub's reactions. It is important to know that clamps are most painful when they are removed. Expect the sub to cry out in pain!

CFNM

CFNM stands for "Clothed Females, Naked Men". It underlines the power imbalance between the Mistress on the one hand and the malesub on the other. While the woman is fully clothed, the man has to present himself stark naked. There are CFMN parties where this fetish is celebrated.

Cock and Ball Torture (CBT)

The term CBT is more or less self-explanatory. It describes the practice of torturing the genitals of the slave. I don't like the term "torture" because I think it's too extreme. Causing pain for pleasure is fine, but we don't want to truly torture anyone. CBT is the generic term with ballbusting as a sub-category. The Mistress can punish the sub's balls and penis in multiple ways: hitting, kicking, pinching, twisting, dripping candle wax, stretching with weights, applying electricity, or rubbing nettles all over them are just a few practices. There are many possibilities to torture the sub's "crown jewels". Masochists can of course be treated quite differently than purely submissive subs, for whom CBT is a harsh punishment. The Mistress can try out different methods to find out which is most suitable for her and her sub. Again, I would like to point out that the Mistress is responsible for the health of the sub and should proceed with caution. Every sub reacts differently.

Since CBT can cause heavy pain, the sub is usually restrained on a St. Andrew's cross or a pulley so that he is at the Mistress' mercy. If you don't have such a thing in your living room, you can also use a sturdy table. The sub is restrained with his back on the table. Now the Mistress can let off steam as she pleases.

The best way to start a CBT session is with your hands. Pinch the sub's scrotum, hitting him on the penis with her bare hand. You can attach weights to shoe laces, which you loop around the sub's testicles. Be careful not to limit the blood flow. Many subs find it erotic when the Mistress wraps up their genitals with a nylon stocking. The stocking is tied in such a way that the testicles are divided and protrude from the body. The penis can also be tied in such a way. When the balls are tied, you can attach weights to them. Start with light weights. As always, pay attention to the sub's reactions and increase the weights slowly.

Nettles on the genitals are good for satisfying the Mistress's sadistic cravings. On contact, the plant's fine hairs prick the skin of the sub and a liquid containing formic acid is injected into the wound. Immediately the slave feels a short, burning pain. Nettles often leave red and swollen marks on the skin that burn and itch. The sensation is very unpleasant - even if it is good for the blood circulation and therefore healthy in moderation. Normally, the burning subsides after about 15 to 30 minutes.

Aloe vera has a cooling and soothing effect when applied to the affected areas. Urine is also often recommended as a home remedy. You can have fun with this and send the sub into the shower or bathtub, where he is allowed to administer his own urine therapy under your watchful eyes. If you have this procedure in mind, it is advisable to let the sub drink a lot beforehand.

Cuckolding

Cuckolding describes a practice in which the Mistress, with the knowledge and support of the sub, has sex with another man (called a "bull"). All the while the cuckold is deprived of sexual pleasure. Often the cuck is kept chaste by the Mistress with a chastity device. This three-way relationship between Mistress, bull, and cuck can take on many different forms. Sometimes there is hardly any contact between cuck and bull, sometimes the bull and the "hot wife" humiliate the cuck together, and sometimes bull and cuck are friends.

There are three degrees of cuckolding:

C1: The cuck still has intercourse with the Mistress, but enjoys seeing his wife occasionally as a "hot wife" with another man.

C2: The cuck has less and less access to his Mistress. His wife has many lovers and lives her promiscuity openly.

C3: The "never-inside-cuck" has no longer any sexual intercourse with the Mistress. The Mistress pleasures herself with lovers, while the cuck is kept in chastity.

To further humiliate the cuck, the hotwife can order the cuck to organise her play dates and pay for the expenses, such as the cost of a discreet hotel room. If the meeting between Mistress and bull takes place at home, the cuck can be ordered to serve the two lovebirds, hand out drinks as well as condoms, and iron the bull's clothes.

Deepthroat

Men love blowjobs. As a sub, however, they enjoy them much less, because now they have to suck cocks themselves. The Mistress likes her strap-on to be sucked and makes sure that the sub performs well. A step up from the regular blowjob is the deepthroat blowjob where the Femdom penetrates nice and deep into the sub's throat. It is also humiliating to playfully slap the sub in the face with a dildo. The Mistress can also tease her slave about how skilful he is and how much fun he obviously has servicing cocks. "You are a real natural! Super. You're doing it really well. It looks like you've had a lot of practice sucking cock..."

Humiliation Games

Many subs long to be degraded in a session. They love humiliation. The Mistress can dish out face slaps, verbally abuse her slave, or use him as a toilet. Inexperienced Femdoms have inhibitions about fulfilling the sub's desire for humiliation. They often shy away from face slaps in particular because it seems too intimate to them. I think it would help them overcoming these reservations if they would recognize that many subs crave humiliation. They love it! Therefore, Femdoms don't have to feel guilty or inhibited when it comes to such games. Once the session is over, however, the Femdom should make it clear in the follow-up conversation that these humiliation games only took place in the context of that particular role-play. After all, there may be subs who ask themselves after the session: Did she really mean what she said? Am I really a worthless worm? To avoid a long-lasting harm to the sub's psyche, the Femdom has to set the record straight afterwards. Experienced players may find this excessive. However, I think it is part of the Femdom's duty of providing decent after-care.

Service

Service can be a fetish in itself. Some subs love to be at their Mistress's disposal and serve her in various ways. They like to serve as a butler, chauffeur, or servant in the household. These men are intoxicated by being allowed to wait on a dominant woman hand and foot. I know of one case where a man in his mid-50s with a characteristic bald head serves as a butler for a tall dominatrix with long brunette hair. He shops for her, drives her to appointments and in return gets scolding lectures about his insufficiencies peppered with face slaps. What an interesting exchange!

Domina's Kiss

The Mistress kisses the slave in her own way. Namely, by letting her saliva drip into his open mouth. In order to humiliate the slave, the Mistress might also spit into the sub's mouth. See also: Spitting

Facesitting

As the name indicates, the Mistress sits on the face of the slave. Usually she is clothed, while the sub is naked and tied up. Especially when clothed, it's fun to feel the sub's desperate attempts to lick you. His failure is inevitable. Again, he proves to be completely useless.

Forced Feeding

Feeding is practice where the sub is forced to ingest food and liquids. This can be done in many ways. For example, the sub can eat from a plate at the Mistress's feet. It gets a bit more difficult for him when he has to eat from a dog bowl. Being forced to eat crushed food from the Mistress's high heels is a more extreme form of feeding the sub. Another interesting option: The sub is fed like a dog, has to do sit up, and beg for treats.

Feminisation / Sissy-Play

Feminisation refers the process of turning the sub into a sissy by forcing him to wear women's clothes. His masculinity is denied and his penis transforms into a clit. Denying a man his masculinity is a particularly strong form of humiliation. Men with smaller penises often have an inclination for chastity combined with sissy play. They love to be trained as whores who have to offer themselves to men on the street. They learn to walk on high heels in an appropriately slinky manner, to dress and apply slutty make-up, and to suck cock. For them, the idea of prostituting themselves for their Mistress is very attractive. In 99% of the cases, however, this happens only in their imagination. According to the new German Prostitution Protection Act, it would also be illegal.

Fetish-Play

A fetish can be almost anything that triggers a sexual reaction in a sub. Very often it is high heels, nylons, or feet. But there are also more peculiar fetishes such as the balloon fetish (looner). It involves the use of balloons. Some people get excited when balloons are blown up, burst, or when they rub against them. The so-called crushing fetish is as bizarre: Observing objects crushed under the Mistress's high heels triggers the sub's sexual arousal.

Figging

The term figging refers to the insertion of ginger into the sub's anus. Ginger is cut into the shape of a butt plug and then carefully inserted into the anus. It burns! As always with such games, I advise you to approach it slowly and not to go all out straight away.

Fixing

Shackles. See: Bondage

Flag

Beating/Whipping. See: Punishment.

Foil Bondage

The Mistress ties up the slave in plastic foil. Once he is immobile and vulnerable he is ready for further manipulation. The area around his penis can be exposed and... well, I'm sure you know what to do next.

Tip: If you fix the sub in a standing position, he might lose his balance and suddenly topple over. This is a very dangerous situation and can lead to serious injuries, since the sub is unable to use his hands to soften the impact of his fall. Keep this in mind when restraining the sub. Hold him firmly and provide sufficient padding around him just in case.

Caution: A sub that is fixed in foil for a longer period of time can suffer from overheating. You must avoid overheating the sub at all costs. Do not let the sub stew for too long.

Foot/Shoe-Fetish

This is an extremely popular fetish. In my experience, almost all subs are foot and shoe fetishists. It is amazing how much time subs can spend admiring the female foot. High heels embody feminine elegance and are therefore well suited to being worshipped by male subs. Most women love to revel in their sub's devotion to their feet, to have them kissed, licked, and massaged. Push your slave to peak performance! Don't settle too quickly. Find out what your sub craves most and offer him this pleasure in return for a good foot massage. What does the sub desire most? Is it gossamer nylons on the Mistress's feet? Is it the long, pointed heel that the sub greedily wants to take into his mouth? Or does your slave love to suck your every toe? Find out and use this knowledge to motivate him.

Get your sub into the habit of always kissing the shoe you put in front. Rules like these help your sub to behave correctly and to find his way around.

Tip: If you enjoy into being worshipped in this way, you can condition the sub to kiss your feet as soon as you snap your fingers. This is fun and thrills everyone watching.

Weights

Weights are used to test the sub's capacity for suffering and to satisfy the Mistress's sadistic cravings. They look good on the nipples and testicles. However, you should never overdo it, because testicles and nipples are sensitive areas. If the weights slip off the nipple clamps, you have gone too far. By the way, falling weights are also a danger to the feet. You can attach the weights to the testicles with a nylon stocking.

Tip: To test how much weight a sub can endure, you can attach a bucket to his balls (a plastic bottle also works). Now slowly fill the bucket with water and watch the sub's reaction.

Gyno Chair

The gyno chair is a useful and entertaining piece of furniture used for clinic games. It is also very suitable for public displays, because the sub is forced to reveal his most intimate parts. On the gynaecological chair, the sub's anus is perfectly accessible, ready to be used.

Urethral Dilation

The Mistress cannot only penetrate her slave anally. Urethral dilation is a practice where the Femdom inserts a sterile dilator into the sub's urethra. The dilator is a metal rod that comes in different diameters. It is especially important to work with sterile dilators and to clean them diligently after use. It can be a lot of fun for the Mistress. Men often compare the feeling of having a dilator in their urethra with the urge to urinate. Urethral dilatation should only be performed by Femdoms who have studied this procedure in detail or have medical training. Performing this procedure requires your full attention. By the way, there are also special urethral vibrators.

Whore Training

A favourite fantasy of many slaves. They imagine having to work for the Mistress as a whore and are trained accordingly. For example, they have to suck the Mistress's strap-on or she takes them anally. See also: Feminisation/Sissy Play.

Imprisonment

A role play in which the sub slips into the role of a prisoner and the Mistress into the role of the strict warden. The prisoner is at the complete mercy of the female warden's whims, who can harass him as she pleases.

Caging

The slave is locked up in a metal cage and has to wait for the Mistress's attention. She can sweeten the wait by inserting a plug into the slave's butt.

Hot Wax

You probably all know the use of hot wax from the film "Basic Instinct". Sharon Stone drips hot wax onto the skin of her play partner and thus inflames his passion for her. Especially in combination with ice cubes, hot wax can be an intense experience.

Do not use conventional household candles. It is better to buy special SM candles, which are available in every well-stocked erotic online shop. These candles have a lower melting point and their wax is not as hot. Also, make sure to hold the candle up high so that the wax has a longer path to the skin and can cool down a bit.

Untrained Femdoms cannot even imagine that a little bit of wax can hurt like hell. Many of them carelessly dribble it onto the man's glans and testicles. For many subs that it way too extreme!

Tip: Try the wax on yourself first before using it on your sub. Get a sense of how much wax can hurt.

Tip: Before using candles, think about how you want to extinguish the burning sensation. Ice cubes, for example, are quite suitable. A warm golden shower is also be a delightful remedy.

Chastity

The Mistress locks the sub in a chastity device. By keeping the keys, she takes control of his sex life. You wouldn't believe how many men love this type of play - but mainly in their heads. Very few subs can really last for several days, weeks, or even months. They exist, but they are rare. I know what I'm talking about, because chastity is a speciality of mine and I have studied it in depth.

For beginners, I recommend increasing the time frame slowly. If you immediately want to spend two weeks in a chastity device, you can easily overexert yourself. Begin with one hour, then several hours, then a day. Small steps lead to the goal, big steps tend to make you lose interest quickly.

A sub wearing a chastity device naturally invites the Mistress to tease and torment him with sexual stimulation. This is great fun! I keep my sub Toytoy captive in a cage and document his chastity on my blog. Take a look at the "My Slave Stable" section if you want to take a look.

Lady-Sas.com

Tickling

Hihihi, tickling gives most Femdoms (and their subs) a good laugh. The sub is fixed defencelessly and tickled by the Mistress at her whim. For example, she can use a feather on the soles of his feet. Some subs last only for minutes and beg for mercy quickly because they can't take it anymore. Other subs, on the other hand, are completely indifferent to it. Conclusion: You simply have to try it out.

Classic Training

In classic training the Mistress is untouchable and physically distanced. There are no intimacies allowed. Usually it is combined with flagellation, spanking, and other forms of discipline.

Medical Play

Medical play is a type of role-playing scenario in which a dominant doctor or a dominant nurse "treats" a submissive patient. Like other role-plays it attempts to be as realistic as possible. Many professional dungeons have their own rooms for this purpose, simulating a real doctor's office. In one common scenario the patient lies naked on a gynaecological chair with a female doctor in a white coat examining his anus with disposable gloves. "You have a stiff limb? I see, well, we'll have to take a look at that right away. But first have to check whether the prostate is enlarged..."

Gags

There are numerous possibilities for the Mistress to gag her slave. She can, for example, use special gag masks. Or she might stuff her pantyhose into his mouth to silence him. Make sure that the sub always has a way to communicate with you and that he can stop the scene if necessary. If he is gagged give him the option to raise his hand or signal in some other way. It is a real nightmare having to endure heavy pain while you are being gagged although you would like to beg for mercy.

Long Term Training

The notion of "long-term" is relative. For one sub, long-term play begins at three hours, for another it lasts at least one day. In professional dungeons, "rest time" is also often included in long-term training. The sub usually "rests" alone in a room, a prison cell, or a cage. A typical offer for a long-term education consists of 3 hours of training and 2 hours of rest time.

Military Drill

In this scenario the Femdom slips into the role of a strict drill instructor who bullies the male recruit. Military games often take place outdoors. The recruit has to crawl through mud, do push-ups, run sprints, and endure nettles. Often, he proves to be completely incapable of following orders and therefore needs to be punished and humiliated. Canings and slaps in the face are common. Obviously, this is not for sissies.

Needles

Ouch! In needle play the Mistress uses needles to pierce the skin, nipples, or even the foreskin of the sub. It should always be carried out with sterile hypodermic needles. On piece of advice: If a sub is drawn to needle play, he should always ask if the Mistress has the appropriate training (nurse, doctor) and knows what she is doing.

Watersports / Golden Shower

The terms watersports and golden shower refer to scenarios involving urination. Many slaves love to feel the Mistress's pee on their body or even swallow it. They serve as a slave toilet. There are specially constructed toilet chairs built for this purpose. The slave is positioned with his head under the lid of the toilet chair. Now, the Mistress takes a seat and pees into the toilet. Her urine is collected in a funnel and runs into the slave's mouth via a hose. The slave might also wear a mask with a mouthpiece that is connected to the hose and to the funnel. Thereby, not a drop of the precious golden nectar is lost. Subs often perceive golden showers as a reward and a sign of distinction. Slaves who are into humiliation also love to be peed on from a Mistress towering over them. Watersports should always be enhanced by proper verbal humiliation. Otherwise, the experience is not as rewarding for the slave. You can for example say something like this:

"Now the Mistress will show you what you are good for. Nothing at all! At best you are good enough to serve me as a pissoir. Yes, slave, now you will be pissed all over. You deserve it. And nothing else."

When the Mistress is finished, she can clean herself with toilet paper and carelessly flick the used paper at the sub. "You stay here until my urine has dried. You will wear the smell of your Mistress's piss for the next few days. Isn't that nice, slave? My nectar will penetrate deep into your skin." Laughing, she can now devote herself to other things while the sub remains drenched in her urine, gradually getting colder. This represents a deep form of humiliation that can trigger the highest pleasure in a slave.

A few more notes on the taste of urine: It is assumed that urine tastes bitter when the Mistress has drunk a lot of coffee. I know a professional dominatrix who eats a particularly healthy diet before she sees a client with an interest in watersports. She eats lots of vegetables and drinks a lot of water to give her pee a nice flavour. Urine is an excretory substance of the body. It is not everyone's cup of tea to come into contact with it. You shouldn't force anyone into it. Wikipedia tells us about possible risks:

"From a medical point of view, fresh urine from healthy people can be handled without any problems. The low concentration of bacteria in urine is due to bacteria living in the urethra; these bacteria

are usually harmless and non-pathogenic for healthy people. Contact with stored urine should be urgently avoided because of the rapid onset of contamination of the fluid. It is possible to contract diseases by ingesting urine from a sick person. (...)"

Ingesting urine is not completely without risk. A Mistress who does not want to pee into her slave's mouth directly but uses for example a dog bowl should not wait too long to serve her urine. Instead she should make the sub drink her pee as quickly as possible, in order to avoid any contamination.

By the way, the intensification of watersports consists in the ingestion of feces ("caviar"). However, I don't want to pursue this topic any further because my aesthetic sensibilities won't allow me. There are slaves who are into it, but you don't have to do satisfy their every whim.

Face Slapping

A slap in the face is probably the quickest and easiest way to make the slave understand his position vis-à-vis the Mistress. In a split second your firm slap emphasizes the power imbalance between you and your slave.

But be careful! Especially for couples, slapping is often a hard limit. There is probably no other punishment that is as personal and intimate as slapping another person in the face. For some people, the face is an expression of the other person's personality, so to speak. And of course, this should be handled with care.

But there are also slaves who love to be slapped and who can't get enough of it. It is important to note that your hand should never hit the ear. Otherwise, the eardrum can be damaged, which is very painful. The Mistress must therefore carefully aim her slaps.

Tip: Put on leather gloves. On the one hand, because your hand won't hurt so much after an intense slap. On the other hand, because leather gloves feel nice but are also tough and nasty.

Tip: For safety reasons, take off all rings when handing out slaps.

Orgasm Control

The Mistress takes control of the sub's sexuality. See: Chastity

Outdoor Training

The attraction of being discovered plays a big role in outdoor training scenarios. It is exciting to take the naked sub for an early morning walk in the forest and lead him on a leash. Hardly anyone really wants to be discovered, but the mere possibility creates a pleasant shiver.

Tip: The sub should get thick, well-padded knee pads. If you have to crawl through the forest on all fours, you need some form of protection.

Tip: What should you do if you suddenly come across hikers? Sometimes it's too late to hide in the bushes. My advice: Keep walking and wish them a good day. Act as if it is the most normal thing in the world to take your naked slave for a walk in the forest. If you are lucky, the hikers will remain cool, greet you back, and move on.

Tip: Avoid contact with children and young people at any cost. Causing a public nuisance is not a trivial offence in Germany. Think about the legal implications before you boldly drop by a campsite. If someone feels harassed and calls the police, you might get sued and/or pay a fine.

Pet Play

Pet play describes a scenario, in which the sub plays the role of an animal. Popular versions of pet play are, for example, puppy play, pony play, and "mock slaughter". As a dog the sub must remain consistent in his role. Does a dog walk on two legs? Can a dog talk? Of course not! The sub acting out canine characteristics needs to undergo a strict obedience training regime. He learns to walk next to the Mistress, to fetch sticks, and to roll over.

"Mock slaughter" is a rare but not uncommon scenario. The Mistress acts like a butcher preparing a pig for its slaughter. This is certainly a very interesting scenario for a psychologist.

Pony play is one of the most common types of pet play. There are special outfits for horses, including bridles, and hooves. The Mistress trains the horse by using various whips and crops. As a horse the sub learns to follow commands and perform different trots etc. Water and hay can be served as rewards.

Pillory

The pillory is commonly known as a Medieval form of punishment. It consists of a wooden rack, exhibiting criminals in the market square. Passers-by could mock and humiliate them. In the context of BDSM it is mostly used as a means to immobilise the sub so that he can be spanked in front of an audience.

Mindgames

Mindgaame are not about physical punishment, but about manipulating the sub's psyche. The slave should get scared, feel panic, or despair. It represents an interesting form of play requiring creativity and imagination. Does this sound a bit too theoretical? Well, here are two concrete examples.

The Mistress ties up the slave in an elaborate bondage in the middle of the living room. Suddenly the doorbell rings. This interruption will hardly leave the slave cold. He will get even more palpitations when the Mistress calls out "I'll be right there" and opens the door. Not knowing what comes next the sub is left to his own devices and desperately tries to process the situation.

For a sub who is not into pain the mere mention of a cane can bring about a similar reaction of terror. The Mistress announces her decision to give the sub a severe thrashing. Her cane hisses threateningly through the air several times only to land right next to the sub but not on his ass. Whew, that was close.

Be careful not to overburden the sub by fucking with his head. A weak heart might not be able to endure it.

Electrical Play

Electricity is used on the genitals and/or nipples of the sub to create different sensations. These sensations can range from very pleasant to extremely painful. There exists a wide variety of electrostimulation devices. A recent invention is that of an electric chastity cage, combining electrical play with chastity training. Especially exciting is the possibility of controlling the level of stimulation remotely.

Role-Play

Role-playing is an essential part of BDSM. It offers adults the opportunity to let their imagination run wild. Who do you want to be? Anything is possible in your imagination. There are no limits. I highly recommend role-playing to everyone, because it works like a breath of fresh air. It keeps the relationship between Mistress and slave exciting and counteracts routine.

Here are some role-play scenarios for your inspiration.

• The Mistress visits a slave market and examines a slave who has caught her attention. Is he qualified to be allowed into her service?

• The Mistress slips into the role of a department store manager who has caught a shoplifter in the act. Now it's time to teach the cheeky fellow a lesson he won't soon forget.

• The Mistress takes on the role of a secret agent who has captured a spy. She interrogates him and uses questionable methods to get him to talk. Who is the mole? Who is working for the other side? The agent is determined to find out and will stop at nothing.

- The Mistress transforms the slave into a TV whore prostituting himself to other men on the street. He needs to be dressed as a slut and receive training in how to properly service the cocks of his suitors.

- The Mistress tests the sub's resilience so that she knows what price she can get for him at the slave market.

- The Mistress takes on the role of a prison warden who humiliates the prisoners and satisfies her sadistic cravings.

- The Mistress is the boss of the sub. She seduces him and turns him into her pleasure slave who has to satisfy her whenever she wants.

- Kidnapping! The Mistress has abducted the sub and is holding him captive in a secret place. She wants to extort a ransom from his wife, while she enjoys training him to be her slave.

- The sub slips into the role of a dog and is trained by the Mistress.

Ruined Orgasm

As soon as the sub starts to cum, his penis is no longer stimulated, jerked, or massaged. He can no longer stop the ejaculation but gets none of the satisfaction that usually comes with an orgasm. His orgasm is ruined. Sometimes a ruined orgasm can even be painful.

Shoe-, Nylon-, and Foot-Fetish

This is probably the most common fetish among submissives. They love to kiss, lick, and worship elegant high-heeled shoes. The same goes for legs in delicate nylons or the bare ladies' feet. Some subs get so lost in their adoration that they can worship the Femdom's feet for hours.

Sensory Deprivation

Sensory deprivation is a type of sensation play. By using a variety of implements like masks, blindfolds, mittens, or headphones the Mistress deprives the sub of one or more of his senses. We perceive the world with our eyes, ears, sense of touch, nose, and taste buds. If these senses are (partially) no longer available to us, we become disoriented and insecure. In the context of BDSM this can have an erotic effect. However, when used over a longer period of time, it can be considered torture potentially causing serious damage. Do not use this type of play for too long and with the necessary respect for your play partner.

Slave Training

The Femdom trains the sub to be her personal slave. In order for this training to be successful she needs to exactly know what she wants and how to get it. So: Please read on diligently, Ladies! Components of slave training are, for example: How do I greet my Mistress? How do I address her? How do I behave in her presence? How can I satisfy her? How can I amuse her? How can I serve the Mistress?

Spanking

Spanking refers to beatings administered to the buttocks or other body parts of the sub. Implements that can be used include the bare hand, crops, whips, belts, etc.

Spikes

Leather belts and harnesses covered internally with sharp metal spikes are often used to punish a slave. Another common application are spiked shoes. With every step of the sub their spikes dig deeper into his flesh.

Spitting

The use of spit during play has at least two dimensions. First, there is the contemptuous spitting in the face, often combined with face slaps. And then there is the so-called "domina kiss," which can be considered to be a reward for sub. He kneels and opens his mouth wide, while the Mistress bends over him and lets her saliva run into his mouth.

The Rack

The very term rack with its Medieval overtones makes one shiver. The use of the rack is almost self-explanatory: The slave is tied by his hands and feet and stretched with a wheel. Today, however, the rack is mostly used to immobilise the sub. His body is not seriously stretched. Once he is helpless a variety of implements can be used on him.

Tease and Denial (T&D)

T&D is a very exciting practice, in which the Mistress arouses the slave until orgasm is almost inevitable. When he is right on the edge of ejaculation she suddenly stops the stimulation and denies him the climax. After he cooled down she starts stimulating him again. The Mistress raises the slave's hopes for an orgasm, teases him until he is close to it, and lets him cool him off again.

In sessions, it is common for the slave to ask permission before an orgasm. "May I please cum, Mistress?" is the correct wording for such a request. It is strictly forbidden to cum without the explicit permission of the Mistress. A slave who dares to do so must be punished. The sub asking the Mistress for permission provides her with the necessary leeway for even more tease and denial.

The trick is to manipulate the sub's hopes. He must always seriously believe that this time he is allowed to have an orgasm. This time I will cum! For sure! His hope is raised and then disappointed. The denial must come as a surprise at the very last moment when he is right on the edge. The closer to the brink he is the deeper the frustration.

Trampling

The Mistress steps on the slave's body and lets him feel her pointed heels. Caution! Pointed heels can be dangerous if you accidentally slip off. I am not a fan of walking on slaves, but there are definitely followers of this practice. As a matter of principle, you should not put pressure on the abdominal wall. Don't get confused by videos in which so-called "Femdoms" in high heels cheerfully trample their slaves. This can end in serious injuries.

"Tunnel Games"

This term refers to a form of play that cannot immediately be stopped once it started. It is like entering a tunnel with the only way out at the end of it.

An example might be a useful illustration: If the sub sends the key of his chastity device to his Mistress in another city, a quick release is impossible. Or: The burning pain of nettles cannot immediately be alleviated.

Verbal Eroticism

The art of arousing a slave with words and to verbally spur his imagination. See chapter "The Language of a Mistress".

Interrogation

The Mistress plays the role of torturer interrogating the slave in order for him to reveal a secret. This presents a nice challenge for her. How much pain, threats, and humiliation can he endure, until he breaks down and reveals his secret? A common role for the Mistress in this kind of play is that of a KGB officer.

Public Display

Slaves who are into humiliation often love to be displayed in front of other people. The Mistress can exploit this inclination and show off her slave to other women. This exposure creates a feeling of strong humiliation and/or arousal in the sub.

I enjoy displaying my slave and have even written a book about it (Title: *Public Humiliation)*. Publicly displaying her sub has great advantages for the Femdom. It is an expression of her absolute power over him. It also creates a feeling of pride of ownership. (Look, he's mine!) Furthermore, it enriches the relationship between Mistress and slave because it provides a welcome breath of fresh air. I usually make a point of really getting to know the audience during the scene. For me, that is really exciting. Before play, I would like to be informed about their interests, but not to the degree that we have nothing new to explore. My main concern is to figure out whether the lady is reliable and will show up for play. Unfortunately, that is not always the case these days.

This is how a typical public display works for me: We usually meet at my house. I let the lady arrive first and invite her in. The slave is not present at this time. Serving coffee and cake creates a relaxed, pleasant setting for the scene. As soon as I notice that the lady is relaxed and ready for the experience, I bring in the slave, who was waiting naked and freshly showered in an adjoining room. I take him by the leash and introduce him to the guest. He has to greet her and present his body in order to be examined. We discuss his physical condition and his training level. Once the initial inspection is over the sub has to show his obedience and perform humiliating tasks for both of us.

Depending on their mood, some ladies get actively involved in the action. Others remain passive the whole time and just watch. Either way, a public display is always a very special event that enriches the everyday life of Mistress and slave. It is highly recommended with the caveat that you should have really settled into your role as a Mistress. There is nothing more embarrassing than a Mistress attempting to proudly show off her slave who stubbornly refuses to follow orders. This is an unpleasant situation for everyone involved.

Wax Play

See: Candle Wax Games.

Smoking Fetish

Some subs find it particularly erotic when a Femdom smokes. Use this fetish to your advantage. Slowly wrap yourself in clouds of intoxicating smoke. My tip: Smoke two or three times as slowly as usual. It looks really sexy!

Maid Training

The sub slips into the role of a maid. He is forced wo wear a maid's outfit and trained accordingly. See also: Feminisation.

Spanking

The favourite practice of many sadists and masochists. When being beaten, the body releases adrenaline and endomorphins. These substances create a pleasant feeling. That's why being beaten often feels so good. Subs often compare the feeling to flying and suddenly being weightless.

Often you will hear the slave begging: "Please, Mistress, more! Give me more!" But the Mistress should think twice about granting this request. Because in the state of total submission, subs are - to put it bluntly - no longer completely sane. They can no longer assess their situation correctly. Therefore, a responsible Mistress stops even when the sub begs her to continue.

The list of spanking implements includes: paddle, crop, cane, single tail whip, flogger, and bullwhip. While the paddle or the crop are also suitable for beginners, inexperienced Femdoms should keep their hands off single tails and bullwhips. The bullwhip in particular can cause significant injuries and should only be used by experienced players. It is advisable to attend a seminar before using a bullwhip.

Please do not attempt to learn from spanking scenes in commercial SM videos. As already mentioned, you might end up watching ladies who have no idea what they are doing. They might just mindlessly thrash the body of a submissive. That is not what spanking is all about! Remember that only the buttocks and the upper back are suitable places for a hard spanking (more on this below).

Important: Before you strike properly, you must first warm up the sub and stimulate the blood circulation. Spank the sub for a few minutes with your bare hand. The buttocks will be supplied with blood and are now ready for other implements. Pay attention to the sub's reactions while you are spanking him. The body releases endorphins during the warm-up, which relieve the pain and can lead to a state of intoxication. An initial effect sets in after about 10 to 30 minutes.

Tip: Slow down the rhythm of your strokes. Enjoy the punishment.

Tip: To get a better feel for the sub's reactions, you can have him count the strokes loud and clear. Listen to his voice. If he sounds close to tears, you can react immediately and slow down. It is amusing to unsettle the sub and ask him if he has miscounted. He is not sure? Too bad, now you have to start all over again.

Tip: While spanking, build up the tension from rather gentle strikes at the beginning to hard strokes at the end. Stick to this routine and it will be easier for the sub to take the beating.

Classification of Strokes: Light, Hard, No-Go

Light Strokes

Light, quick blows can be administered to the belly and the chest. The forearms and shoulders as well as the sub's private parts are also possible areas. But be careful: light means that the blows should not be too painful. This type of spanking is more about the psychology than causing actual physical harm. Anything else can lead to injuries.

Hard Strokes

The Femdom may hit the buttocks hard. The upper back as well as the upper arms and the upper and lower legs can also be attacked vigorously. All these areas can take a heavy beating because of thick layers of fat under the skin.

No-Go Areas

Never strike individual bones or vertebrae. This can lead to permanent damage. For this reason, the head and neck, spine, and joints are completely off limit. Hard blows to the genital area are also prohibited.

Forced Ejaculation

The Mistress forces the sub to cum, although he may not be allowed to do so.

Forced Feeding

The slave is forced to ingest certain substances. This can be a bowl filled with the Mistress's urine or other substances that the sub finds revolting. As part of medical play, the patient can be forced to swallow fluids through a tube.

Lesson 7.

How to Come Up with Creative Ideas for Your Session.

A good session is based on imagination and creativity. It is not about working through as many practices as possible but about expressing yourself. Your approach going into the session therefore should be as playful as possible. Think of the session as a kind of wonderland, in which you can realise almost anything you want as long as it does not cross the hard limits of the sub. In this wonderland there are only two enemies: boredom and risk. You must learn to deal with both of them. By boredom I mean: don't let a routine develop. Every session should be unique and surprising. With risk I refer to the inherent dangers of some of the more intense practices. BDSM is not without danger, so you should minimise risks and dangers. Is that difficult? No, not with a little practice.

There are Femdoms who are bursting with ideas. And there are Femdoms who are rather uninspired and nervously ask themselves: What am I going to do in the session? I have no ideas, I just can't think of anything exciting. Don't panic, let me provide you with some ideas to get started.

The Mechanics of Imagination:
"Carrot and Stick"

Ask yourself what your sub desires most. Now think about how you can utilize this desire and tease him with it. For example, if your sub has a fetish for leather boots, attach one end of a leash to his testicles and the other end to a heavy table. Now step in front of the sub in sexy leather boots and instruct him to greet you. While your slave enthusiastically worships your boots, slowly move backwards - until the sub has to stick out his tongue to reach the coveted boots. His testicles are stretched while he is desperately trying to reach the object of his desire. How amusing! Enjoy watching the sub's tongue fighting for every inch and the slave's balls being stretched out.

Think of other ways how you can place his fetish in front of him in a teasing way. For example, how about ordering the sub to get on all fours? Take a seat on his back and instruct him to greet you. Try it out! You will find that it is impossible for the sub to reach your boots in this position. The sub cannot obey your command even though he tries really hard. His failure gives the Mistress reason to mock and then punish him for his disobedience.

The mechanics of imagination works like this: In a first step figure out what the sub desires. And in a second step think about how you can make it difficult for him to fulfil his desires.

The Idea of a "Challenge"

This is a different method helping you to spur your imagination: Think in terms of challenges! What challenge could you present the sub with? What obstacle can you think of that he would have to overcome? What test of courage or skill comes to mind?

• For example: How about leading the sub around on a leash? He is instructed to keep it taut at all times. No sagging allowed! Move around the room and suddenly take a step towards him. There is no way for him to prevent the leash from sagging - oops, he already lost.

• Or how about this challenge: Is your sub capable of inserting the whole heel of your boot into his mouth?

• Will he manage to drink a whole bowl of urine within 10 seconds?

• Is he brave enough to go into the Ladies' room of a restaurant and take a photo of himself there?

The method here: Think about challenges.

The Idea of "Surprise"

Another possibility: What would your sub definitely not expect from you? Disorient him by acting unpredictably. Use the element of surprise. Surprises keep every relationship alive. Be creative and give it a try!

For example, if you are extremely discreet and generally avoid public S&M parties, even though your sub would like you to try it out, then lose your inhibitions and organise your own S&M party with a couple of friends.

If you are aiming for a pure S&M relationship without vanilla sex, then tantalise him by not wearing panties under your leather skirt.

If you have always refused to slap him, surprise him and conduct an interrogation peppered with hefty face slaps.

I know that you first have to overcome your inhibitions, break away from old ideas, and courageously enter new territory. But it's worth it. Surprises are great!

The Method: Think about the sub's perception of you. How can play with his expectations? Overcome your fears and reservations and just do it!

Tip: Always be open to ideas from other people. Get inspired by exchanging ideas with other Femdoms. If you are open-minded, you will never run out of ideas that you can incorporate into a session.

Lesson 8.

Concrete Ideas

for Your session.

If you are new to BDSM it is helpful to have some concrete examples for guidance. In the following I have put together ten interesting suggestions for your session.

1st Idea: The Secret Inscription

Use a marker and write something on the slave's back in such a way that he cannot possibly read the text. Now the two of you visit a Femdom party or a private gathering with one or two girlfriends. The slave will not be able to stop wondering what you have written on his back. In addition, you can always fuel his curiosity with hints: Well, if the other Ladies find out about you, then... well, I wouldn't want to be in your shoes....

Or: What I wrote on your back is sooooo embarrassing!

Or tell him just before the party: I don't think I should have written that on your back after all. I think I went too far.

However, do not change the inscription. That will drive the slave completely crazy. A real mindfuck.

Of course, your behaviour might turn out to be exaggerated beyond measure. Maybe it only says something harmless like "I am Lady X's slave".

2nd Idea: The Impossible Blowjob

The Mistress instructs the slave to suck her strap-on cock and make it squirt. But the sub doesn't seem to succeed. Of course, a strap-on can't squirt at all, but that's part of the fun. The Mistress pretends to be disappointed with the sub's efforts and his inability to bring her cock to a climax. She verbally humiliates him and encourages his increasingly desperate efforts with her riding crop.

3rd Idea: The Bell

Attach a small bell to the slave's chastity device or any other body part. You can for example tie it to his nipples or testicles. The slave is instructed to prevent the bell from ringing. Not the slightest noise must be heard.

Now make him crawl across the room to fetch something for you. Every time the bell rings, he will be punished.

Of course, you can easily make the bell ring by "coincidentally" stepping on the sub's hand. Trust me, despite his best efforts you will be able to make the bell ring!

4th Idea: The Clothes peg Challenge

Set your slave the challenge of attaching 30 clothes pegs to his cock and balls. Increase the number from session to session until he is unable to attach any more pegs. He is punished accordingly.

Variation: In a second step you can whip off the nasty clamps with a riding crop. This is painful and you have to aim well. However, you should not be put off by the slave's whining. If your strikes are hard and precise everything will go well.

5th Idea: The Seat Cushion

Use the slave's face as your seat cushion (this is also called facesitting or queening). Decide how much air you grant the slave. It totally depends on your mood. This type of play is particularly interesting if the slave has been in chastity for a while and is therefore extremely horny.

While you make yourself comfortable, you can leaf through a magazine, for example. Of course, it is important to pay close attention to signals from the slave so that he is not harmed in any serious way. Lack of oxygen can be very dangerous. Try to pay careful attention to the slave's reactions and still pretend that you hardly notice him.

Whether you wear a leather skirt, pants, panties, or go completely naked is entirely up to you.

6th. Idea: Push-Ups

There's nothing more exciting than a muscular, well-trained slave! Increase the sub's fitness by making him do push-ups. Make it difficult for him and sit on his back.

Variation: Stand in front of the slave and give the command to perform push-ups. With each lowering of his body he must kiss your left and right shoe.

7th Idea: The Dildo Challenge

Insert a dildo into your slave's ass. Please make sure that the dildo is nicely lubricated and slippery. The slave is faced with the challenge of keeping the dildo in his ass-pussy. It must not slip out under any circumstances! The more gel you use, the more difficult the task.

Now the slave receives a second order. For example: Clean the floor in the kitchen, slave! Or: Crawl around me and kiss my high heels from all sides, slave!

If the dildo slips out, he will be punished. If you want to increase the difficulty, you can also put a dildo in the slave's mouth.

8. Idea: The Sex Doll

Forcing the sub to fuck an inflatable sex doll is very humiliating. He is not good enough for a real woman. Sex dolls are available in almost all sex shops. The more crude and vulgar the doll, the more humiliating it is for the sub. You can give the doll a name and declare her the slave's girlfriend.

You can increase the intensity by combining this scenario with a public display. The slave is first shown off and then mounts his "girlfriend", the sex doll, at the end of the session. This is extremely embarrassing!

9th Idea: The Yes Man

The slave may only give one answer to all your questions: "Yes, Mistress". This results in amusing situations.

For example, ask:

"Slave, would you like to be fucked really hard today?"

"Are you a stupid fool, chasing every skirt?"

"Are you ashamed of your little mini dick?"

And so on.

Do not use this game to go beyond the sub's limits. A no-go remains a no-go.

10th Idea: Seamed Nylons

Seamed nylons not only look erotic, they're also great for a little game focusing the slave's attention. Instruct your sub to kiss your stockinged legs from the bottom to the top along the seam. If the slave's lips touch any part other than the seam, he will immediately receive a resounding face slap.

It is amusing to slap him even though he followed your orders to the dot. Too bad for him! By refusing to admit his failure, he only makes things worse for him and punishment is even more severe. In the end, he has no choice but to apologise for his clumsiness.

Further Reading

You can find more ideas and inspiration in my book "200 Ideas for BDSM Session".

Lesson 9.

Your Equipment.

BDSM can be a very expensive hobby - but it doesn't have to be. These days there seems to be an infinite selection of fetish clothing, toys, and SM furniture. When I am in Hamburg, I often visit the Boutique Bizarre on the Reeperbahn. Not necessarily to buy much, but mainly to be amazed again and again by the sheer size of its selection of SM gear (Note: I mention the Boutique Bizarre without any quid pro quo, this is not meant as an advertisement).

My tip: Feel free to browse. Let yourself be inspired and discover something new. But remember: You don't need everything you can buy. In fact, you can get by with just a few essentials. **You already have the most important equipment for a successful session. It sits right between your shoulders. Yes, that's right, I mean your brain.** Imagination, creativity, and desire are key ingredients for truly legendary sessions. None of these ingredients are for purchase. But don't worry: with this book, you'll be well on your way to getting a good dose of knowledge as well as inspiration. In the following, I will recommend a number of toys for beginners and advanced players. At the end of this section I will give you tips on where you can make good purchases.

Which Basics Do I Recommend?

Let's start with the **outfit**. I don't want to bore you with tips on clothes and make-up. You know your own style better than I do. Stay true to yourself. Wear something that feels sexy. I do have one tip though: almost every sub I know is into high heels. It would be unwise not to exploit this fetish. High heels have an extremely strong appeal. Slaves love it when their Mistress shows off her high, pointed heels. They love the smell and shiny surface of the leather. My advice: Do your sub a favour and wear high heels. Stockings have a similar effect on men. They are turned on by the sight of a woman's leg wrapped in nylon. Use your feminine charms to captivate the sub. Eroticism has its own rules, but it would be a mistake not to utilise them. So, when a prospective Femdom asks me for outfit tips, I tell her to wear an outfit that she finds sexy as long as it includes should include stockings and high heels.

There may be some readers who would like to receive even more detailed advice on this topic. They might be tearing their hair out in front of the wardrobe. For these readers I am happy to give a personal assessment. Everyone else can skip the following paragraph. I don't want to bore or lecture anyone.

From my experience I know that submissive men in their role as slaves often find the contrast between naked slave on the one hand and clothed Femdom on the other very stimulating. This means for your outfit: Don't show too much skin! A nice well-fitting pencil skirt with stockings and high-heels combined with an elegant white blouse looks classy and feminine. You can hardly go wrong with such an outfit. I personally find an outfit that is too revealing rather inappropriate since it blurs the contrast between naked slave and dressed Femdom.

When it comes to **SM equipment,** I advise you to purchase the following **basics** (depending on your inclinations, of course):

- 1 x paddle

- 1 x crop

- 1 x strap-on (small diameter)

- 1 x collar with leash

- 1 x knee pad for the sub

What? That's it? But yes! With these five basic items of equipment you are ready to go. You don't have to spend a lot of money to have fun. My advice: Buy less, but buy better quality.

Let me briefly explain the basic tools. The knowledge necessary to use a paddle and the crop correctly can easily be acquired even by beginners. Both implements cause mild to severe pain and are therefore ideal for familiarizing yourself with different spanking techniques. The intensity of the pain can be controlled well. A bullwhip, on the other hand, should not be put into the hands of a beginner, because it is dangerous and can lead to nasty injuries. It would be irresponsible to use such a whip without expert training. In short: You are well served with a paddle and a crop for the time being. You can purchase other implements once your skill and confidence have increased.

Whether you get a strap-on depends on whether you and your sub are into anal play. I highly recommend this toy to Femdoms though. It's a great feeling to reverse the roles and savour the power of being able to penetrate the male body. You should definitely give it a try! I would also like to encourage men to try it at least once. There is nothing gay about being impaled with a strap-on. Rather, it is a sign of openness, confidence, and courage. I disagree that you are only a good and well-behaved sub if you like strap-on play. It is absolutely fine, of you don't like it. Every Femdom has to respect the sub's limitations. But it's definitely worth a try.

I find that a collar and leash is a beautiful symbol of the slave's submission. It expresses his devotion and his trust in his Mistress's leadership.

Finally, I would recommend a set of knee pads for all slaves – not only those over 50 or with bad knees. Anyone who thinks "Oh, that's only for wimps" has certainly never spent an hour on his or her knees, crawling around on all fours. Believe me, well-padded knee pads are extremely helpful for the sub to enjoy the session.

What Do I Recommend for Advanced Players?

Once you have acquainted yourself with the basics and would like to progress further, I recommend the following list of implements for advanced players:

- 1 x flogger

- 1 x cane

- 1 x nipple clamps

- 1 x strap-on (larger diameter)

- 1 x anal plug

- 1 x hand and foot cuffs

- 1 x spreader bar

- 4 x bonding ropes

- 1 x candle

- 1 x dog bowl

The flogger can also be considered to be a basic piece of equipment, but I find that in the beginning you can limit yourself to just two striking instruments. The cane is a cruel implement causing intense pain. You should use it sparingly and not immediately go all out unless you want to scare off the sub. Some beginners might think about buying a cane cheaply. I advise against this. Many of these canes are of low quality. They splinter easily and the sub can get injured. My general advice: Buy few but high-quality toys that meet all safety requirements.

Nipple clamps are not absolutely necessary. Clothes pegs will do although they have the disadvantage of looking rather bland. Therefore, they do not contribute to the creation of an erotic atmosphere. Nipple clamps made of shiny metal have a very different effect. By the way, subs react very differently to nipple torture. Some can take a lot, while others are extremely sensitive.

A strap-on with a larger diameter and an anal plug make sense when Mistress and slave have taken a liking to anal play. You should insert the plug at the beginning of the session (or even before to increase the anticipation). The anus is thus already stretched and ready to be used. Advanced anal play almost always involves an increase of the strap-on's size. To be blunt: it becomes longer and thicker. The sex toy industry caters to these tendencies. There are strap-ons that have the size of a human arm. Some of you may wonder whether it is realistic to anally insert such monsters. Simple answer: Yes, it is. There are slaves who have been stretched to the point where they can take gigantic cocks. Such subs often also enjoy fisting, i.e. being penetrated with the fist (in disposable gloves and with plenty of lubricant). Such extreme practices are not for beginners. And whether it is desirable to be stretched out in this way is something each sub must decide for himself.

Hand and foot cuffs, spreader bar, and bondage ropes help to render the slave defenceless.

Finally, wax play can bring additional heat into the scene. As already mentioned: Please do not use ordinary household candles or the remains of the Christmas wreath. Instead purchase specific SM candles with a low melting point.

If you still have room in your budget, you can also buy a dog bowl, which is readily available in supermarkets. You can use it for all kinds of watersports.

Lesson 10.

Safety and Communication During the Session.

Do you know the most important word in BDSM? It is "no". After all, we are talking about scenarios where you can quickly overstep the other person's boundaries. But that must not be allowed to happen. The Mistress must always respect the hard limits of the sub. If she does not, she risks losing his trust. This can be the beginning of the end of the relationship. Is it worth it? I don't think so.

To prevent such a negative outcome from happening, clarity is of the utmost importance. **It must be completely clear and unambiguous between the two of you what is possible and what is not.** The sub must be absolutely honest and not try to impress the Femdom by claiming to have little or no hard limits. Negotiate the scene openly.

In practice, I often observe couples who think they have clearly discussed their preferences and limits but in reality, they have not done so at all.

Misunderstandings and mutual reproaches are inevitable. What to do?

I recommend writing down preferences and no-gos with bullet points, so that there are no ambiguities. Even better: Pin this list to the wall so that you are constantly reminded.

Many slaves think that Mistresses demand absolute silence during a session. Surprise: That is not the case at all. It is true that a sub should only speak after being spoken to. Chatterboxes are disrespectful. But: That doesn't mean that the sub should remain totally passive all the time. It is no fun to play with a man who shows no reactions at all. That's terribly dull. **It is the reactions of the sub that make play so appealing and interesting for the Femdom.** Reactions are not limited to words. They can also be expressed through facial expressions, gestures, and moans. Non-verbal communication is essential.

Is the rope bondage too tight? The pain-distorted face and strained panting of the sub might give you an indication. Is the rope too loosely attached? The sub looks impassive. Develop a sense for these nuances! Yes, it's all about psychology. **A good sub gives feedback to the Mistress using facial expressions and gestures, not by mouthing off.**

Saying No

The Mistress should always offer the sub the possibility to communicate his mental and physical state. **In my opinion, a sub must be able to interrupt play or ask for mercy at any time.** In BDSM circles there is a lot of discussion of so-called safewords. If the sub utters a certain word, such as "mercy" or "exit", the Femdom must immediately stop the action. The argument "But before the session you were explicitly agreed to this" does not apply. A sub has the right to change his mind at any time. He might suddenly realise that a golden shower is not for him even though he expressed interest beforehand. The Femdom needs to respect the sub's physical and emotional boundaries at all times. These are the rules of the game. The sub must always have the opportunity to make himself heard. If he is gagged, he must at least be able to shake his head, raise his hand, or waive. There is nothing worse for the sub than to be pushed beyond his limits without any ability to beg for mercy.

In practice, I often observe subs who suffer silently without speaking up. They grit their teeth because they want to impress their Mistress. This is a commendable attitude, but I would advise against it. If the sub feels physical or emotional discomfort he should speak up. A responsible Femdom will respond to the situation. After all, the session should be fun for everyone involved. An alternative to the safeword is the traffic light system. Green means: Everything is okay. Yellow means: Slow down, I am reaching my limit but do not break off the session. And red means: Stop the session immediately. Of course, you can develop your own sign system.

Another common issue is the reluctance of couples to communicate openly with each other. They find it embarrassing to freely discuss their desires and fantasies. It should not be that way. One possible solution: Those who cannot talk about their desires can fill out a questionnaire.

Here is an example of such a session questionnaire for subs. It is far from complete and anyone can modify it, including their own interests.

Slave Questionnaire

I consider myself a (tick or circle as appropriate): sub, slave, pet, sissy, property, cock girl, whore, own description:

I would like to be addressed as:_____

I am submissive, masochistically inclined.

My submissiveness on a scale from 0 (not at all) to 10 points, (very pronounced):
____ points

My masochism on a scale from 0 (not at all) to 10 points (very pronounced) ____ points

I am straight, bi, bi-interested, homosexual.

Bi active, bi purely passive, bi active & passive, don't know yet.

Physical limitations:_____

_____

My fitness level on a scale from 0 (not at all) to 10 points (very much): _____Points

My no-gos_____:

_____

_____

_____

_____

_____

_____

_____

My interests:

(Mark with a cross or circle where applicable):

- Genital Bondage
- Anal stretching
- Anal fisting
- Anal plugs
- Spitting
- Human Ashtray
- Breath Control
- Blindfolds
- Ballbusting
- Bastinado
- Punishment
- Nipple Play

- Bondage
- Nettles
- CBT, Cock and Ball Torture
- CFNM, Clothed Female Naked Man
- Anal Stretching
- Deepthroat / Blowjob
- Humiliation (light / medium / heavy / extremely heavy, physical / verbal)
- Crossdressing
- Facesitting
- Feeding
- Feminisation
- Fixation
- Flag (soft / medium / hard / extremely hard)
- Foil bondage
- Weights (namely here:_____)
- Gynaecological chair
- Urethral Dilation
- Whore Training
- Cages
- Chastity Device (Model: _____)
- Tickle Torture
- Classic Slave Training
- Medical Play

- Gags
- Long-term Training
- Military Drill
- Needles (and here:_____)
- Face Slaps (soft / medium / hard / extremely hard)
- Orgasm Control
- Outdoor Training
- Pet Play (Dog / Pig / Horse _____)
- Pillory
- Mind games (_____)
- Electric Play
- Role-play (_____)
- Ruined Orgasm
- Shoe, Nylon and Foot fetishism
- Sensory Deprivation (masks)
- Sissy Training
- Slave Training
- Spanking (beatings with hand, whip, crop, cane, clap, strap, belt, _ _____)
- Spikes
- Boot Fetish
- Boot kicks (soft / medium / hard / extremely hard)
- Rack

- Strap-on (small / medium / large / extremely large)
- Trampling
- Toilet Training (golden shower / caviar)
- Tunnel Games
- Verbal Eroticism / Dirty Talk
- Interrogations
- Public Display (in front of:_____)
- Wax Play
- Diaper Fetish
- Smoking
- Maid Training
- Forced Ejaculation
- Forced Feeding

Additions and comments:___

_____

_____

_____

_____

_____

_____

In the session, I prefer to wear:

_____

_____

_____

I would like my Mistress to wear the following:

_____

_____

_____

When I jerk off, this is what I fantasise about:

_____

_____

_____

_____

_____

_____

_____

Tip: Give the sub ample time to fill out the list of interests and go over the information together with him. It is best to do this at the beginning of the session. It helps the sub enormously if he is in his slave role during the discussion. It is often psychologically difficult for subs who have to stand their ground in everyday life to suddenly switch to their slave role.

Who says that only women are complicated? Okay, you don't have to understand that now, but take my advice to heart and go over the questionnaire with each other at the beginning of the session so that there are no misunderstandings.

Golden Safety Rules

Safety in BDSM is an important topic about which one could write a separate book. However, I would like to give you a few golden rules.

- Sterilise your toys after each session to minimise the risk of infection.

- For CBT and CBB: Pay attention to the colour of the testicles. If they are dark or bluish in colour, you should release the bondage immediately. Another indication of problems: The scrotum feels cool to the touch.

- When playing bondage games, you should always be prepared to release the sub quickly and safely in case of an emergency (e.g. have a suitable pair of scissors at hand. Try them out beforehand so that you know how to use them).

- Hit the buttocks, they are well padded. Don't hit sensitive areas like the genitals or the stomach too hard. Don't be confused by S&M videos where Femdoms do just that. It is dangerous and grossly negligent.

- Do not apply pressure to sensitive areas such as the neck or the abdominal wall.

- When you slap the sub in the face, be careful not to hit the ear. Aim for the cheek. If you hit the ear with full force, serious injuries like a burst eardrum can occur.

• Never leave a bound slave alone. Think with me! What happens if the sub's blood circulation suddenly drops and he collapses? Always anticipate such a scenario and be ready to react.

• Does the sub have heart problems or other health restrictions? The sub did not mention anything? Yes, but did you actively inquire about his medical condition before the session? As a Femdom you are responsible for the sub's health. Take this responsibility seriously. Only do things to him that do not put a strain on his health.

• Make sure that the temperature of the play space (including the floor) is comfortable for a naked sub.

• Make sure that the sub can always communicate. Never gag him in such a way that he cannot make himself heard, if he reaches his limits. The sub must have the possibility to abort the session at every moment. Do not hesitate. If he wants to stop, you must act immediately.

• Breath-taking looks are fine. But taking the sub's breath away as part of a breath reduction play is a dangerous tightrope walk. Rather stop too early than too late.

- **Do not listen to the sub when he asks for "more". He does not know what he is doing at that moment. It is your responsibility to protect the sub from himself.** This is true for all types of play and not only for extreme practices like breath reduction. I read about a professional dominatrix who strangled her client to death because she followed his requests. Of course, the dominatrix was taken to court.

- Say no to drugs and too much alcohol. You should not be intoxicated during play.

- If, despite all precautions, there is an accident, call for help immediately. You are still wearing your latex dominatrix outfit and your sub sports his leather outfit? Doesn't matter! It's a medical emergency. Get help. Don't hesitate. Take responsibility and act.

"Covering"

What does the word covering mean? The phrase "I'm going to get covered" describes a safety mechanism. You let yourself be protected and safeguarded by a third party, while you are on a date. It works like this:

1. Ask for the phone number of your date. If he or she does not give you the number, this is a reason to cancel the meeting.

2. Check whether the number is correct by simply calling back. For example, ask to clarify an unanswered question.

3. Be upfront about being covered at the meeting.

4. Give the phone number of a trusted person. SM groups in large German cities also often do cover work. Agree on a time when you will call the trusted person.

5. If you do not call at the agreed time, the trusted person will call the number and demand to speak to you in person in order to make sure that everything is okay. It is important that your confidant does not take no for an answer. According to the motto: Yes, everything is fine, she is just using the

bathroom. If the person of trust does not manage to get a hold on you in person within a very short time, he or she will call the police.

Both Femdoms and subs should get covered. Especially when you don't really know the other person yet. Don't make the mistake of listening to your gut. My ass: It feels alright! Or: Oh, he's so submissive, he'd never dare touch me. That attitude can change dramatically very quickly. It's better to be on the safe side. Getting covered doesn't cost anything, but comes with the advantage of security. That is priceless.

Lesson 11.

Sexual Gratification.

Now let's turn to the climax of the session: the orgasm. The Mistress always decides who comes when and how.

The Orgasm of the Femdom

One of the most common questions I hear is whether it is a dominant Mistress should have sexual intercourse with her sub. Am I not giving up power when I let the slave fuck me? Many women build up sexual tension during S&M play and wish to release that tension by fucking the slave at the end of the session. However, I often hear from Femdoms who never feel 100% comfortable having intercourse with a sub. My answer to this is clear: **Yes, it is absolutely fine for a Mistress to fuck her sub**. If the Mistress feels like it, she should do it without any remorse.

However, there are a few things to keep in mind. It would be wrong to suddenly give up the reins and not be dominant anymore. A woman who has just been the strict dominatrix and now suddenly kneels in front of the slave to suck his cock will naturally have to cope with a loss of power. She might even appear as inauthentic. It's not about her sucking the sub's penis. It's about how she does it. All Mistresses have sexual needs and it is healthy to satisfy them. **However, it is important to always make it clear to the slave that the Mistress is only using him to satisfy her needs.** He is like a sex toy. She uses him for her pleasure and determines if, when, and how sex takes place. If the sub feels that the Mistress continues to hold the reins and guides him, everything is fine and the Mistress does not lose any of her authority.

In concrete terms: Always keep the upper hand. Tell the slave clearly what he should do and what you expect from him. Particularly refined Mistresses deliberately set very high expectations and always show themselves dissatisfied with the sub's performance. This is a trick to avoid giving the slave the satisfaction he longs for: Wow, I was really good and did a great job for my Mistress. Such a feeling can easily lead to inappropriate, arrogant behaviour. Consider this: Praise for a very good performance is not wrong, but it should be rare. Praise very, very little. This makes it all the more valuable and the sub will try harder next time.

An acquaintance of mine, let's call her Silvia, trained her slave to lick her as soon as she snapped her fingers. Unfortunately, the relationship is over but she still raves about how exciting it was.

There are Femdoms for whom it would never be an option to be sexually satisfied by a sub. They can only have sex with a partner with whom they see eye to eye. And that is a bit difficult when the sub licks your shoes and kisses your ass.

An intermediate solution is to train the sub as a sex toy while not giving him any sexual pleasure. You can for example put him in a chastity device and have him wear a dildo gag in his mouth. Now you can have him kneel in front of you and let him pleasure you. The Mistress climaxes, the sub does not. Worse still for him: his cock languishes in the cage while the Mistress enjoys herself.

Of course, a Mistress is free to choose how she wants to climax. She can also decide that after the session she will enjoy regular vanilla sex with her partner. Why not? Whatever pleases her is permitted. But again, my tip is: keep the reins and order the sub around. Guide him and never let him make decisions. You are the Mistress - even during sex.

So-called classic dominatrixes do not allow any direct physical contact. The only way for the slave to have an orgasm is by jerking off. He masturbates in front of the dominatrix - of course only after she has expressly allowed him to do so. In addition, the sub must explicitly ask for permission to cum.

A nice but also nasty way to milk the sub without giving him sexual pleasure is the so-called ruined orgasm.

The Ruined Orgasm

A ruined orgasm in the context of BDSM means an ejaculation without pleasure. At the moment of the climax the orgasm is purposely halted. The slave is brought to the point of no return where the sexual pleasure is at its highest and where the orgasm is triggered. From this point on there is no way to stop it. But if the stimulation abruptly ends the ejaculation takes place without any pleasure. By not being allowed to touch himself anymore the sub's cock begins to squirt, creating an absolutely unpleasant feeling, often even associated with some slight pain. It could have been so beautiful! But alas, how frustrating! Having to come this way is absolutely no fun for the sub.

One way to trigger a ruined orgasm is by tying the sub to a St. Andrew's cross with hand and foot cuffs. The Mistress jerks his penis and stimulates him until he squirts. She can also use a vibrator. As soon as the slave comes, she takes her hands or the vibrator off his cock ruining the orgasm.

Another possibility: The slave lies on his back and jerks off. His hands are tied with ropes or chains. As soon as he comes, the Mistress pulls his hands away and the orgasm is ruined.

A ruined orgasm brings no real satisfaction for the slave. Many Mistresses love it and enjoy the sub's frustration.

Forced Orgasms

A forced orgasm describes an orgasm that is beyond the control of the sub and against which the sub cannot defend himself. For this kind of play it is helpful to first impose a strict ban on orgasms and then stimulate the sub with a vibrator until he can no longer hold back. Tie him up and spur his imagination by telling him what he will have to endure if he dares to come. The fun consists in watching his futile attempts to control himself.

It is really evil to continue teasing the penis after the orgasm as if nothing had happened. The cock gets overstimulated and starts to hurt very quickly. Allow yourself to have fun and pretend you didn't notice the sub's orgasm. Keep stimulating him and see what happens. Don't worry: It usually hurts, but it's not dangerous.

Finally, I would like to emphasise that it is not necessary for a session to end with an orgasm at all.

In conversations with many professional dominatrixes I have learned that there is quite a number of subs for whom an orgasm is not important. For them, it is more about role play and the feeling of being able to block out everyday life for a while. They want to spend some carefree time in a fantasy world and recharge their batteries. Everyday life will return soon enough.

Prostate Milking

Prostate milking is another interesting form of forced orgasm. It can also be called prostate massage. It involves the Femdom using her fingers to stimulate the prostate to such an extent that the slave releases sperm. One cannot speak of a real orgasm. It is more like a "leakage" or a "milking".

The prostate (prostate gland) is a gland that produces about one third of the sperm. The Femdom can feel it when she inserts a finger into the sub's anus. The prostate gland can be felt after about 10 cm with the finger pointing towards the abdomen. Since the gland is extremely sensitive, she must be particularly sensitive when touching it. It requires a sure and sensitive handling of the situation.

How-to Guide

1. The slave empties his bladder and bowels.

2. The Femdom informs herself about the anatomical details of the male body so that she can locate the prostate (google helps). She puts on a disposable glove and applies a copious amount of lubricant.

3. The sub is on all fours. The Mistress gently penetrates the slave from behind with one finger.

4. The Mistress now carefully tries to find the prostate. It is located about 10 cm towards the abdomen and is about as small as a walnut.

5. Found it? Great. The Mistress now massages the prostate gland with her finger, applying constant light pressure. She can let the finger circle and move it slightly up and down.

6. If everything goes well, the Mistress feels the prostate swell and begin to vibrate.

7. Communication with the sub is important, so the Mistress is informed about the state of the sub's arousal.

8. The sub is leaking sperm. His pleasure in doing so is very limited.

9. Now is the time to verbally humiliate the sub and play with his mind.

A prostate massage can be an extremely pleasurable affair, because the Mistress can extend the sub's pleasure for a very long time. She can also delay the ejaculation and give him a long, very intense orgasm. But here we are not talking about a "prostate orgasm". Instead we discuss prostate milking, i.e. making the sub leak his sperm with very little pleasure.

Lesson 12.

Ending the Session.

Everything beautiful comes to an end. In professional domina studios, most sessions end with the client's orgasm

"As soon as the client has cum, I have no more power over him," explains a dominatrix friend from Hamburg. For her it is quite clear that the slave is only allowed to cum at the very end of the session. She continues: "Men who have come often don't feel like playing any more. Their horniness makes them do everything I want. But when they are not horny anymore, I lose my power." For clarification: An average session in a domina studio lasts one hour.

As already mentioned, I recommend not to end the session abruptly, but to let it end with a ritual. The experience should be allowed to reverberate for a while. To abruptly tear a sub out of his fantasy world is like a shock. It is comparable to waking up: We know we're going to wake up, but we're not 100% there yet, we're still yawning, rubbing our eyes, maybe we need a coffee first. A Mistress ending a session abruptly is like someone pouring a bucket of water over our heads and drive us out of bed. That's very unpleasant. I prefer to let it end slowly and gently.

Sure: Capping the session with an orgasm at the end is an excellent idea. But the motto "cum, shower, and get out", that is common in some bad domina studios is simply wrong. Give the sub some time to slowly say goodbye to this bizarre world. For example, have him lick your boots in detail once more. Such rituals are important to ease the farewell and to provide stability for the sub's fragile state of mind.

A sentence "You may say goodbye now, slave," might introduce such a ritual. He must crawl to the Mistress, kiss her high heels, and thank her for the session. The Mistress takes the collar off the sub and the session is officially over. Both assume their normal personas, talk to each as equals.

Now is the time to check whether the sub has sustained any injuries that need to be treated (disinfected).

The Follow-up Conversation

Now is the time to relax, take a shower, and then have a debriefing. In this post-session conversation, both partners can openly talk about what they liked and what they did not like. It's not easy for a Femdom to switch back into her normal persona. This is where a self-assured Mistress excels. **You have to be able to handle criticism.** No one is perfect and constructive criticism is an integral part of a good follow-up conversation. I know from my own experience that it's not always easy, because you still feel like the infallible Mistress. You think: What? How? I try my hardest to put on a super session and this ungrateful bastard dares to criticise me? And because of such a triviality? Outrageous! This is an insult to my majesty!

But criticism is good. It helps us grow and get ahead. Praise doesn't help me develop as a Femdom, criticism does. So be smart and listen as calmly as possible. If the criticism upsets you emotionally: take a deep breath, count to three, take another deep breath, force yourself to smile - and then respond. Think of it as an exercise in self-control. I know very well that people are quick to take criticism personally. After all, it's about personal behaviour. But I find it helpful to realise that criticism is necessary in order to be able to develop. If you react emotionally and indignantly to criticism, the sub may never dare to criticise you again. This will hurt you in the end. Because, as I said, praise does not help you grow.

Of course, the Femdom is also allowed to voice her opinion and inform the sub about what she liked and what she didn't like. She is also allowed to criticise. Now is also the right time to evaluate whether you are on the right track with your long-term goals for the slave. Was it a step forward or a step back? What does this mean for the next session? Take a moment to reflect.

Tip: Always start with the positive. Even if there is one point that you noticed in a very negative way, don't let this negative experience cast the whole session in a bad light. See the positive first and appreciate the nice experiences. Try to praise the sub. But also avoid letting negative aspects fall under the table. A sub has a right to receive honest feedback.

Catching Up After the Session

After particularly intense sessions, the sub may need special attention. If you notice that he is visibly shaken, trembling, or weak it is time to embrace him, offer him support and security. You don't have to say anything. Just holding him tight can make a big difference. Give him the feeling that you are there for him and that you value him as a human being. Take as much time as necessary.

Often one speaks of the sub being "caught" by the Femdom after the session. This is a beautiful image. It is your job to catch him. Make sure that the sub stands firmly on both feet when he returns to his daily life. Is there still a need to talk? Does he still have something on his mind? Listen carefully and don't hesitate to ask.

Humiliation games in particular should be properly addressed after a session. The Mistress should emphasize that she only tried to fuel his imagination. It is important for the sub to understand that the Mistress respects and values him and sees him as an equal human being. The impact of humiliation games should not be underestimated. There are subs who are excellent at distinguishing between play and reality.

Unfortunately, there are others who continue to ask themselves after the session: Wait a minute, did she really mean it? Is it really true what she said about me? Am I really a nobody? Many psychological problems can arise from such questions. Therefore, it is necessary for the Femdom to address this issue in the follow-up conversation. Do not wait for the sub to raise the topic. Be proactive! This is part of your responsibility as a Femdom.

Hygiene

Clean the toys you used during the session with a disinfectant. It is available in any drugstore. You should disinfect everything that has come into contact with bare skin. Implements like dildos or strap-ons require an especially thorough cleansing. Make it a habit to clean as soon as possible after the session. It's a bit of a nuisance, but there's no way around it.

Lesson 13.

Personal Development.

When you start out in BDSM, everything is new and exciting. You live in the present and do not think about the future. At least that's how it was for me. But once you have found your way around in this strange, bizarre world you can start to think long-term. As a Femdom, you should ask yourself the following questions: **Where do I want to go with my sub? What development do I want for the sub and what development do I want for myself?**

These are big questions to which there are no quick and easy answers. It is rather an on-going process of self-reflection, developing a vision of your future growth. Only those who have a clear goal in mind can achieve it. If you just play around, you might not make any great leaps forward. I'm not saying that you necessarily have to develop. There may be subs and Mistresses who are not interested in personal growth, and who are content with bringing a little variety into their sex life now and then. There is nothing wrong with that. But there are certainly also many players who, like me, think that it's part of human nature to want to develop. This chapter is aimed at these subs and Femdoms.

The advantages of developing a vision of the future for the Femdom and her sub are obvious. **A Femdom leads. The question is: Where to?** She needs a direction and a goal to be a leader. A sub also needs to know where the journey is going. Defining common goals strengthens the bond between Mistress and sub.

You have no concrete ideas yet? Don't worry, that is quite normal at the beginning. Once you start the process of self-reflection many paths for you and your sub will open up. And even if you do not know how to achieve your goals right away, I would like you to keep them in mind.

Here are some examples of goals you can set for yourself and the sub.

Goals for Femdoms

Lady M. dreams of training her sub S. to be an obedient slave who carries out all of her instructions without hesitation. Finally, she would like to show him off at a private Femdom party. She wants to grow into a self-confident, sovereign Mistress who can't be shaken by anything.

Mistress H. aims to put her sub in chastity and to completely control his sex life. In addition, she wants to feminise him and train him to become a submissive sissy. She wants to develop herself into a cuckoldress who enjoys sex with other men while the sissy languishes in her cock cage.

Mistress A. sees her future self as an accomplished, sadistic leather Mistress who is a virtuoso with all spanking implements - even the bullwhip. She wants to train her sub to become a pain slut who endures even harsh punishments without any whining and begging for mercy.

You see: all the examples are short and simple. It is about the development from the current status quo to a desirable state in the future. Think about it! What kind of development do you see for yourself? Set a goal for yourself and your sub and you are ready to go.

The Session Log

One important tool for achieving your goals is the session log. It is like a notebook in which you can write down your goals or visions. You can also jot down brief descriptions of all your sessions. It is a task that can also be delegated to your sub if you wish. This way you keep track of the present situation and simultaneously remind yourself of your goals. After all, you can only achieve your goals if you don't lose sight of them. Oftentimes goals are not achieved simply because the Mistress didn't think of them at some point. If you are interested in a session log, you can check out my version available on Amazon. It is entitled *BDSM Session Book: Femdom & Malesub. How to Never Forget a Session Again.*

The Slave Contract

In advanced S&M relationships, a slave contract defines goals and stipulates rules and responsibilities both partners have to adhere to. The contract is not legally binding. But it still provides Femdom and sub with a clear set of standards and obligations.

The content of the slave contract can be very detailed or more general. Almost all aspects of your relationship can be regulated, if you wish. I like to give an insight into the set of rules between my slave Toytoy and me. It is only an example. Every slave contract should be negotiated individually.

But before that, I would like to impart ten facts you should know about slave contracts in general.

1. A Slave Contract Provides Clarity

The main reason for me as a Femdom entering into a slave contract was that it clearly defines the role of Mistress and slave. The sub cannot talk himself out of a punishment by claiming "I didn't know". Nor can he refer to the fact that circumstances were "not so clear". That's the great thing about a contract: it states clearly and in black and white how the relationship between the Mistress and the slave is structured.

2. A Slave Contract is Not Legally Binding but It Has Similar Effects

Sure: You don't have to be a lawyer to know that a slave contract is not legally binding. For example, if the contract prohibits the slave from having an orgasm without permission and he violates this rule, there is no legal redress. You can't go to court and sue him. That is ridiculous. In purely legal terms, a slave contract is worthless and you can't enforce it.

From a purely emotional point of view though, a slave contract can still be effective. I have heard from my slave that he feels much more bound to me by the contract than without it. Here the emphasis should be on how he "feels". A slave contract is an emotional obligation that one enters into. In other words, a slave contract helps the slave to focus on his tasks and duties and creates a feeling of obligation.

On a very basic level it remains true that BDSM is a game between adults, played by both sides in complete agreement and without coercion. This statement of mutuality is the basis for everything.

3. Witnesses Make A Slave Contract More Binding

Toytoy and I both solemnly signed our slave contract in the presence of a witness (Lady Cornelitas). It is worth turning the signing of the contract into a small ceremony. You don't have to overdo it, but you really shouldn't sign the contract as if you are on the run. The festive atmosphere and the presence of witnesses add value to the slave contract. I recommend, for example, classical music, candlelight, a great meal for the Mistress and her witnesses and a kinky session for the slave.

4. A Slave Contract Needs a Clear Structure

A good slave contract needs to be clear and distinct so that is easy to comprehend. Leave out any superfluous language. I think it important to have a good outline before you draw up the contract. This is how I structured our contract:

- Purpose and Subject Matter of the Contract
- Rights of the Mistress

- Duties of the Mistress

- Rights of the slave

- Duties of the slave

- Special points

- Exclusivity

- Chastity of the Slave

- Public Display

- Reticence

- Discretion in Public

- Household Chores

- Body Care of the Slave

- Clothes

- No-Gos

- Photos and Videos

- Financial Interests

There are hardly any limits to the content of the contract. Just ask yourself what is important to you and how you would like to structure the interactions with your sub.

5. A Slave Contract Also Lists the Duties of the Mistress

Yes, ladies, being a Mistress means taking responsibility for the slave. That is why a good slave contract also contains the obligations of the Mistress. After all, a slave contract is not a one-way street, but a give and take. My duties in the contract with Toytoy are the following:

<<The Mistress must take care that the slave does not receive any permanent marks in the course of his training and must ensure that his health and anonymity in public are guaranteed at all times. Damage from third parties must be conscientiously averted by Lady Sas. She is responsible for the health of the slave. The Lady also has the responsibility to protect the slave from himself if he is overzealous and takes on too much. >>

Accordingly, these duties are mirrored in the item "Rights of the Slave":

<<The slave has the right to physical integrity and health. He has to endure marks caused by his training, but permanent marks are inadmissible and off limit. The slave has the right to refuse orders if this would endanger him. He is also allowed to

refuse an order if it threatens to out him in public. He may also resist if a command violates his hard limits. The slave may not be punished for refusals of this kind. The slave has the right to ask the Mistress at any time if he may use the bathroom. The Mistress assures the slave that he may exercise his profession and his public social life freely and without any interference. >>

6. A Good Slave Contract Protects the Slave

You may have been surprised to read under point 5 that the slave contract protects the slave from the Mistress. I consider this to be an essential part of any fair slave contract. The Mistress also has to abide by agreements, rules, and obligations. The contract clearly defines limits and protects the slave: "He may also resist if a command violates his hard limits. The slave may not be punished for refusals of this kind." I think it is wise for the Mistress to have her powers limited in this way.

7. A Good Slave Contract Limits the Power of the Mistress

If you are looking for an all-powerful, no-limit Mistress who is allowed to do everything, you don't need a slave contract. A contract formalizes your commitment to each other. It defines Mistress's and slave's rights, duties, and responsibilities. The slave has the right to refuse a Mistress's command if it violates the terms of the contract. This formal arrangement provides security for the slave because the chance of the Mistress overstepping a hard limit has been minimized. He can feel comfortable that his boundaries are being respected. Some may object that a formal contract is not needed to ensure a healthy power exchange. My slave Toytoy though has assured me that after signing his contract his trust in me has increased.

8. A Slave Contract Is of No Use If It Is Not Enforced.

There is a big difference between formulating a contract and its implementation. What is the point of the best slave contract if no one abides by it? The real work only begins after it has been signed. Now the Mistress has to make sure that she enforces all clauses of the contract. I recommend to address this issue IMMEDIATELY. Do not wait and say: Well, he (the slave) can be excused for not adhering to the contract because he still needs to get used to it. Don't make any excuses for him. If you don't take immediate action, you will lose your authority. I recommend for you to IMMEDIATELY insist on precisely adhering to the contract in all points without compromise and exceptions.

9. A Slave Contract Needs to Be Reviewed Regularly

I also recommend that you make sure that both partners review the slave contract on a regular basis. You can place it in the playroom and make it a habit of going over all clauses before each session.

Strict Mistresses often order the slave to learn the contract by heart. This can be difficult but also all the more entertaining if the contract contains a large number of clauses.

10. A Slave Contract Should Not Be Signed Too Early

A slave contract is something special and only appropriate for established Mistress-slave relationships. It makes no sense to enter into a slave contract after only 14 days. This early in the relationship its trajectory is still uncertain. On the other hand, you don't have to wait as long as I did... I cannot recommend a specific time. It really depends on the individual circumstances but you should wait at least for a few months before you decide to formalize your relationship. After all, the slave contract is also a sign of a long-term commitment.

An Exemplary Slave Contract
Purpose and Subject Matter of the Contract

The slave contract is made between Lady Sas and slave Toytoy on Sunday, 29 May 2016. The witness present is Lady Cornelitas.

The contracting parties are aware that the contract has no validity in a court of law. Rather, the contract is intended to set out in writing the rules that have emerged between them since February 2011 and to make them clear to both contracting parties. The contract formally regulates the relationship of both contracting parties, which has existed since February 2011. It is an SM play contract between adults, concluded of their own free will. The contract also serves to officially document that the slave is the property of the Mistress.

Rights of the Mistress

Lady Sas has the right to train the slave as she sees fit. She may use all types of punishment as long as they do not violate the slave's hard limits (hard limits: see below). She can humiliate the slave as she pleases. Lady Sas can demand absolute obedience and submissive, respectful behaviour from the slave. The Mistress has the right to use the slave for work of all kinds, for example in the household.

Duties of the Mistress

The Mistress must ensure that the slave does not receive any permanent marks as part of his training and must ensure that his health and anonymity in public is guaranteed at all times. Damage from third parties must be conscientiously averted by Lady Sas. It is her responsibility to protect the slave from permanent bodily harm. The Lady also has the responsibility to protect the slave from himself if he is overzealous.

Rights of The Slave

The slave has the right to physical integrity and health. He agrees to accept any punishment the Mistress decides to inflict as long as it leaves no permanent marks. The slave has the right to refuse any command that would endanger him. He is also allowed to refuse the order if it threatens a public outing. He may also resist if his hard limits are to be violated. The slave may not be punished for refusals of this kind. The slave has the right to ask the Mistress at any time if he may use the bathroom. The Mistress assures the slave that he may exercise his profession and his public social life freely and without interference.

Duties of The Slave

The slave is aware at all times what a privilege it is to serve Lady Sas. He has to follow orders immediately without hesitation and questioning. It is the slave's duty to make Lady Sas's life more pleasant and please her to the best of his abilities.

The slave must always address Lady Sas formally and with respect. This also applies to all other Femdoms whom the slave might encounter. He must behave according to the customs of a classic Mistress-slave relationship, including slave positions, greetings, etc. The slave must always behave in such a way that the Mistress is proud of him. Outside observers should be able to notice the many years of Lady Sas's training. The slave has to limit contact with the Mistress on weekdays to an absolute minimum so that she can fully focus on her profession and her social life.

Exclusivity

The slave binds himself exclusively to Lady Sas. He is her slave and property. He is not allowed to have sexual or any other contact with other Femdoms. This applies especially to professional dominatrixes. The slave is expressly forbidden to approach, write to, or otherwise contact other women. He must immediately forward any contact requests he might receive to Lady Sas.

Lady Sas, on the other hand, is not exclusively bound to the slave. She is free to meet others as she pleases and bring them into the relationship at will. She is also allowed to play with other subs in the presence of the slave. The slave must accept this without resentment or jealousy. He expressly acknowledges that he is nothing more than a slave of Lady Sas who serves her only in the context of an SM play relationship. He is not to be considered an equal partner of Lady Sas.

Chastity

The slave grants Lady Sas complete control over his sex life. He has no right to an orgasm. Lady Sas controls the slave's sexual drive and has the right to keep the slave chaste by using a chastity device.

Lady Sas has to ensure that she always keeps a spare key to the slave's chastity device in her home. The slave is not allowed to free himself from the chastity device or to manipulate it in any way. Both parties agree that only Lady Sas determines whether or not the slave is allowed to climax. The slave has the right to ask the Lady for an orgasm. He has the right to receive a decision from the Mistress on the same day.

Lady Sas has the right to lend the key of the chastity device to other Femdoms without his approval

The Mistress has the right to publicly document the slave's chastity in her blog.

Public Display and Entrusting Slave to Others

Lady Sas has the right to publicly display the slave and to give him to others. In this case, the slave is as much subject to these Femdoms as he is to Lady Sas. Lady Sas is absolutely free in her decision to whom she gives the slave and does not need his approval.

Lady Sas must ensure that the slave is not outed in public. Maskless public displays in front of larger groups of eight or more people, e.g. at play parties, must be discussed with the slave in advance. If the slave does not agree, Lady Sas has to accept his decision and may not punish the slave for it. Lady Sas may give the slave to other people only if these people can handle this responsibility, do not pose a danger to the slave, and know and observe his hard limits.

Secrecy

The slave allows the Lady Sas to extensively document his training in books and in her blog. The Mistress may not publish anything that reveals the identity of the slave. Lady Sas is also free to share information about the slave's training.

The slave, on the other hand, is not allowed to publish or discuss any details about his training and his experiences with Lady Sas at any time, unless she grants him permission to do so.

Discretion In Public

If Lady Sas and the slave are in a public setting, they both must ensure that their special relationship goes unnoticed. Exceptions must be discussed in advance and are only allowed if both parties consent. If the slave does not consent, he may not be punished for it.

Household Work

The slave must carry out all household chores carefully, quickly, and enthusiastically. The bedroom of Lady Sas is off-limits. He can only enter after receiving explicit permission. The slave is not allowed to rummage through Lady Sas's possessions, open drawers without permission, etc. The slave has no right to expect anything in return for his service. The slave must take care that the neighbours of Lady Sas do not notice his presence. He must be discreet at all times. If the telephone rings, he must not answer it. If the doorbell rings, he must withdraw.

Body Care of the Slave

The slave has to make sure that his body is fit, attractive, and well-groomed. He has to exercise daily and go to the gym three times a week for one hour. The slave may eat white flour products and sweets in moderation once a week. For the rest of the week he must avoid any sweets. The slave is required to visit the hairdresser regularly and to take care of his body. The slave's genitals and anal area must always be clean-shaven. If the slave violates any these of these rules, he must immediately report it to the Mistress.

Clothing

The slave has to keep his body clean. Before serving Lady Sas he is required to take a shower. He performs his household chores naked, only wearing a collar and knee pads. The Mistress may dress as she wishes. Lady Sas assures the slave, however, that she will consider his high heel fetish.

Hard Limits

Caviar, medical play, permanent marks, outing in public, needles, cutting, hard ballbusting and hard kicking, slaughter games, waterboarding

Photos and Videos

Lady Sas has the right to take videos and photos of the slave's training. She also has the right to show these recordings to others, as long as the slave's face is not visible. The Mistress must handle the videos and photos of the slave with great care and make sure that the slave remains anonymous.

Financial Interests

Both parties agree that they have no financial interests vis-à-vis the other.

Signed on 29 May 2016

Lady Sas, Slave Toytoy, Lady Cornelitas (Witness)

Lesson 14.

Finding a Play Partner.

Unfortunately, finding a suitable play partner is not as easy as finding a tennis partner. To be honest, it is really hard! But it's not so hard that you shouldn't try. Please don't be put off by the negative reports in some publications and internet forums. Just because others have found it difficult doesn't mean it has to be the same for you. Take me as an example. I was lucky enough to meet my slave Toytoy on the internet. It can work. Maybe even faster than you think.

Offline Search

In many cities there exist regional BDSM support and social groups that meet regularly. It is easy find them using Google.

Muster up your courage and attend one of their meetings. Are you worried that someone might recognise you? Or that you might run into a co-worker? I can sympathize with your trepidations. A possible solution: If you live in Stuttgart, why don't you visit the regional group in Heidelberg where no one knows you? If you live in Hamburg, then join to the regional group in Bremen.

BDSM parties are also a possibility. You can meet like-minded people at **play parties** or other **Femdom events.** Just google the city you are looking for and add "BDSM," "Femdom," or "SM party".

Online Search

If you prefer to keep your inclinations to yourself and don't want to join a group, you will find many options on the internet. To German readers: I recommend the website **joyclub.de.** You can find me there under my nickname: LadySas. I don't get anything in return from Joyclub for this recommendation. I just think that it is an interesting community. There are numerous virtual groups where you can exchange ideas. Its members are - as far as I can see - mostly civilised and interesting.

fetlife.com in an interesting international website based in the US. I am registered there as well. Take a look. There are many appealing profiles.

Finding the Right Play Partner
10 Tips for Malesubs

Many submissive men dream of being at the feet of a Mistress. But in most cases, this proves to be anything but easy. This is no surprise if you study some online profiles. It is absolutely clear to me why these men are not successful. In the following, I have compiled 10 tips for willing subs on how they can improve their chances.

Tip 1

Many slaves make the mistake of making everything about THEMSELVES: I have these particular desires! I want this! I want that! **It makes much more sense to focus on the wishes of the Mistress.** Make it clear to her what SHE gains from taking you on as her slave. What are her benefits? You have so much to offer? Great, but what specifically? Put yourself in her shoes and read your message from her perspective. Would you write back in response? Maybe you can do better? Is there something you can do to make her curious?

Tip 2

Make it clear to her what is **special about you.**
Why should she choose you out of the flood of
applicants? What is it that makes you different and
appealing? You can't think of anything? Then I
would suggest for you to sign up for a massage
course, join a fitness club, or take a photography
course...

Tip 3

Do not underestimate the power of visuals. **Sexy
photos are a plus**. But please do not send pictures
of your dick. That is not sexy at all, it's low class.
Women know pretty well how male genitalia look
like, thank you very much.

Tip 4

**Don't present yourself as worthless or without
having limits.** Slaves who pretend that they would
do anything and attach no value to themselves are
not appealing to Femdoms. Men who are quite self-
confident but are be willing to submit to the right
Mistress are much more interesting. Femdoms love
the challenge of being "the right one" for that type of

confident, self-assured sub. One more comment about slaves who claim to have no limits: No one believes you! No slave has no limits. Anyone who describes himself in those terms raises suspicions about their trustworthiness.

Tip 5

Set up a **meaningful profile.** Don't overload it. The main goal is to provide a brief but meaningful representation of yourself. No one wants to read novels or your complete autobiography.

Tip 6

Take the initiative. Write to the lady of your choice. Respond to **her individually**, referring to information from her profile. Don't bore her, **be witty and keep it short**. No one reads more than four or five sentences.

Tip 7

Dominant Ladies receive a lot of mail. They can't reply to everyone. A simple "Hi, how are you?" is therefore not enough to get their attention. Come up with **something intelligent/funny and you'll have a** better chance of getting a reply. Make an effort!

Tip 8

Show genuine interest. In my case I can tell whether someone is genuinely interested if he engages with my blog. It shows me that he made his homework, so to speak.

Tip 9

Accept a rejection like a man. Don't be upset if a lady responds negatively or not at all. There are still many women out there who would love to hear from you. Think positively!

Tip 10

Stay relaxed. Try to see BDSM dating for what it is: a game for adults. Some play it very well, others don't. But it is always good to know a few rules.

Finding the Right Play Partner
10 Tips for Femdoms

Many men think that it is very easy for a Femdom to find a submissive partner. That is not entirely true. Sure, you can find a play partner very quickly. But Femdoms are not just looking for any play partner; they are looking for a very special one. And those are rare. Here are 10 tips for Femdoms which will increase their chances to find Mr Right.

Tip 1

State clearly that you are looking for a play partner. Describe as clearly as possible whom you are looking for. Don't expect to be simply "found". Try to tell potential suitors exactly what you are looking for.

Tip 2

High expectations are good. Why would you settle for just any sub? But please be realistic. Unfortunately, good-looking millionaires with a six-pack, long hair, and a philosophy degree are not a dime in a dozen. Especially when they are supposed to have a cute cat and good listening skills, be funny, can give excellent foot massages, and blindly obey your every order. Keep it real.

Tip 3

Photos, photos, photos! Set up a meaningful profile and be sure to post a few photos that will make slave hearts beat faster. Men are visual creatures. They look at photos first. And only if they like the photos, they will read the text. No photo, no application.

Tip 4

Be sure to touch on some topics in your profile that make it easy for subs to relate to. This makes it easier for them to write a meaningful letter to you. Just tell a bit about yourself as a person.

Tip 5

Be communicative and open. The sub dared to call you by your first name in his message? Be generous and don't throw the email away straight away. Please do not forget that you are a woman first and a Femdom second. I cannot comprehend why some Femdoms want to be treated as a goddess and diva right from the first contact.

Tip 6

Choose carefully. But meet as soon as possible once you find someone interesting. Unfortunately, practice shows that even the most promising candidates mysteriously disappear when things get serious. It's better to find out early then to engage with someone for a long period of time only to be disappointed in the end.

Tip 7

Learn about the sub's desires as quickly as possible. What are his sexual fantasies? What does he dream about when he jerks off? If you know this, you can shape your training accordingly.

How do you find out? You can ask him directly or give him the task of writing down what goes through his head while he is jerking off. On the one hand, it is very direct and blunt, but on the other hand, it poses a delightful challenge for him.

Tip 8

Do not grant the sub an orgasm in the first session and watch closely how he reacts. Does he get angry and act inappropriately towards you? Then he might not have fully understood the dynamics of a Femdom – malesub relationship. His suitability is at least questionable. After all, a good sub understands that it is all about his Mistress and not him.

Tip 9

Even if you have no experience with chastity yet you should at least aim at bringing this practice into the relationship. You will gain a lot of power and the sub will be much more loyal to you. Suggest this possibility early on and observe how he reacts.

Tip 10

Have the sub give you his mobile phone. If he hands it over, he has nothing to hide. It is the ultimate proof of trust. But if he refuses, he probably has something to hide. Now your task is to figure out the reason for his hesitancy. Is he visiting porn sites? Are there email exchanges with another Femdom? Or even a wife? Try to find out.

Lesson 15.
Happiness in BDSM.

SM is a fascinating and bizarre world. In fact, it is so unique, magical, and multi-layered that one runs the risk of losing oneself in it. In short, it's **easy to lose perspective and overdo it.** Slaves often act without any restraint, always looking for the next more exciting kick. The harder, more extreme, and kinkier the better. There is nothing wrong with wanting to develop further. But everything needs to be measured. Personally, I don't think much of a sub striving for lifelong chastity proudly declaring that he has been chaste for years. I also think it's excessive to put yourself in a 24/7 TPE dependency as a slave. It is appealing to be able to relinquish control to your Mistress for a few hours. But there is one thing you should never relinquish: your ability to judge rationally. It is never a good idea to give up common sense completely.

My advice and my request: **Find the right balance.** Harder and faster does not always equal better. Only do what you feel comfortable with.

Confront your play partner if he is out of control. As a Mistress you have to protect your sub from himself. But sometimes you also have to protect Femdoms from themselves. Gently remind them that they are not flawless goddesses, nor princesses or queens, but real women playing certain roles for limited periods of time. It is completely nonsensical to get on a high horse and insist on adoration and subordination even in everyday life. You can do that if you aspire to completely immerse yourself in this lifestyle. But if you conceive of BDSM as one element of your erotic life among others, then you have to learn to be able to switch back to "normal" everyday life.

I don't want to prescribe anything to anyone. Everyone is free to pursue his or her own happiness. However, I take the liberty of warning against a dangerous tendency of mistaking the fantasy world of BDSM for the real world.

Finally, I'll let you readers in on a very important secret. There are some players – often beginners – who believe that they will find happiness and the complete satisfaction of all their desires in BDSM. They become obsessed. Their style of play becomes more and more extreme, their ideas more and more outrageous, because they believe that it will bring them closer to their goal. But they never find bliss. They think it is right around the corner but it always remains just out of reach.

Ultimate happiness is like the carrot the donkey sees in front of its nose: unattainable, but tempting. In my experience, you can't find it by intensifying your style of play. Extreme BDSM is not a direct path to happiness. Happiness has nothing to do with only satisfying your desires. This type of satisfaction is fleeting. It is comparable to the purchase of material goods, possessions, and beautiful experiences for yourself. This happiness is only short-lived because it is a mere accumulation of objects and experiences devoid of any internal value. Bought a convertible? Great, but after a year it has to be a new sports car. You booked your vacation on the Maldives? Very nice, but next year it has to be Hawaii. Four days in a chastity? Cool, but now it has to be seven! We always want more. That's human nature. But we won't achieve happiness that way.

Rather, we become happy when we make others happy. What makes us happy is what we can do for others, not for ourselves. It is better to give than to receive. Here you have it. This is what it's all about. By doing something selflessly for others you will not only make them happy but also yourself.

For a sub, there is nothing more rewarding than making his Mistress happy. For a Mistress, on the other hand, there is nothing more exciting than giving the sub what he needs and to cherish his submission. It is a win-win situation. If you think about it in these terms, BDSM can definitely make you happy. So, my final advice is: **Don't think too much about yourself, think about your partner!** I wish you a lot of fun!

Cordially,

Lady Sas

PS: I hope you enjoyed reading this book and that I was able to inspire and help you. I would be happy to receive your personal feedback. Feel free to write to me at dearladysas@gmail.com or leave a book review on the platform where you bought it.

Femdom Academy, Part 2: BDSM Next Level.

You got appetite and now you want more? Then I look forward to seeing you again at the second part of the Femdom Academy. In the Femdom Academy 2 the further development to the Next Level is the focus.

Glossary/terms

24/7 - a concept that originated in the US. Mistress and slave stay in their roles 24 hours a day, 7 days a week.

St. Andrew's cross - a large cross in the shape of an X. Usually the St. Andrew's cross is attached to a wall. The slave wears hand and foot cuffs and is thus fastened to the cross so that he is rendered immobile and at the Mistress's mercy. He is now ready for nipple play, CBT, or other torments.

Breath reduction - the Mistress controls how much oxygen the sub can inhale. For example, via facesitting.

BDSM - Literally: "Bondage & Discipline, Dominance & Submission, Sadism & Masochism". A general term for playing with dominance and submission.

Greeting - the slave kisses and licks the Mistress's shoes. He starts with the shoe the Mistress puts forward.

Mindfuck - the feeling of being completely wiped out and finished by mind games. The sub feels ultimately taken away. A mindfuck pushes the sub to his psychological limits. For example, the Mistress takes photos of the sub in compromising situations, although it is his hard limit to be outed in public. There is just one detail, the sub is not aware of: There is no memory chip in the camera.

Get "Covered" - a technique to protect yourself from assault during sexual or non-sexual encounters. In a nutshell, you give a friend the phone number of your date and agree on a time when the friend will be called. If this call is not made, the friend calls the number in order to get the person to be covered on the phone. If necessary, the friend calls the police.

Cuckolding - the woman has sex with another man and cuckolds her husband (cuck), who is aroused by this humiliation.

Dilator - medical device made of metal for stretching the urethra.

Dominatrix Kiss - the Mistress lets her saliva drop into the open mouth of the sub who is kneeling in front of her. She can also spit in his mouth (spitting).

D/s - Dominance and Submission refers to the power relationship between two partners on a psychological level. The sub submits to the Mistress. This power dynamic can also extend into everyday life. It does not necessarily involve kink or SM play in a narrower sense.

Facesitting - the Mistress sits on the slave's face, thereby controlling his breath (this is also called queening).

Flag / Flagellation - the severe spanking of a sub. For example, with a cane or a whip.

Pulley - an SM device designed to lift up and stretch a bound slave. Like on a St. Andrew's Cross he is now immobile and can be punished.

Humbler - also known as a "testicle pillory". A device in which the testicles are clamped so that they are exposed and stick out backwards towards the buttocks. Well suited for CBT because of the easy accessibility and sensitivity of the balls.

Chastity belt - a type of chastity device preventing the sub to pleasure himself and keeping him chaste. Abbreviation in German: KG.

Love swing - a free-floating device that is attached to the ceiling. It puts the sub in a reclined position, exposing his genitals and his bottom increasing accessibility for CBT and anal play.

Golden Shower - urine

RACK concept - Risk-aware consensual kink. Both partners are aware of the risks they both take consensually.

Pegging - anal penetration of the sub, for example with a strap-on, a dildo, fingers, or the fist.

Pet Play - the slave slips into the role of an animal, such as a horse, a pig, or a dog. The Mistress treats him accordingly.

Queening - the Mistress takes a seat on the sub's face (breath reduction).

Safeword - a word set before the session that the sub can use to stop play. The word "mercy" is often used. It is also called a code word.

Session - an SM date, where two or more people play with each other.

Slave – submissive who submits to a dominant person as part of a role play.

Slave position / basic slave posture - typical posture for a slave that expresses his submission. Kneeling upright, legs slightly spread, hands resting on the thighs with the open palms facing upwards, gaze lowered submissively.

Slave toilet - a special SM toilet reminiscent of a regular toilet seat. The head of the sub is placed inside the device so he can receive the Femdom's golden shower.

Small Penis Humiliation (SPH) - humiliation based on the (supposedly) small dick of the sub. The actual size of his penis is irrelevant. Even subs with normal or even large penises love SPH.

SM Party – a party that is specifically organized for practicing SM. There is usually a dress code. Large parties often have several separate playrooms.

Spanking - the slapping of the buttocks.

Spitting - spitting on the sub.

SSC concept - principle that games should only be conducted in a safe, sane, and consensual manner.

Strap-on - an artificial cock that the woman can strap on with a harness (strap-on dildo).

Sub - submissive

Switch - a switch alternates between the role of top and sub.

Total Power Exchange (TPE) - a concept that involves the total exchange of power. The Femdom takes complete power over the sub. TPE can cover all aspects of a relationship, including money and finances. Often, the 24/7 concept is used instead of TPE but they are not synonyms. The difference is that TPE describes the intensity of the submission and 24/7 the duration.

Topping from the Bottom - the sub tries to influence and control the actions of the Femdom from his subordinate position (wish list slave).

Vanilla - a person who does not practice S&M. The term is often used somewhat pejoratively. Like the word "Muggle" in Harry Potter ;-)

Farewell - the slave kisses and licks the Mistress' shoes. He starts with the shoe that the Mistress puts forward first.

Wish list slave - a sub who wants to dictate to the Mistress how she should conduct the session (topping from the bottom).

Contact and Feedback

I'd also be very interested to know how you like the book. Write to me personally at my e-mail address dearladysas@gmail.com or leave a review on amazon.

I also invite you to visit my Femdom blog, where I have put together many interesting interviews with professional and private dominas for you (many of them in English) and also present my own point of view:

Lady-Sas.com

> – *Many thanks to Jörg for proofreading. You were a great help to me.* –

More from Lady Sas

I have recorded my experiences and the education of my personal slave Toytoy in some books. They have been published on amazon as paperback and eBook. Search amazon for the keyword "Lady Sas" to get my books displayed. For example:

Suddenly Domina – my secret life as a private domina

This book tells how it all began. Lady Sas is a private BDSM Mistress from Frankfurt in Germany. In her book she allows the reader to share her private BDSM play, and provides a graphic and vivid description of how she trains and uses her slave. (Not for faint-hearted readers!) The narrative and literal climax of the book is her joint session with Lady Cornelitas, in which her slave is taken to his physical and psychological limit – and even beyond...

Chastity Belt Training 1: 7 days kept chaste with tasks from Lady Sas

You dream of being kept chaste in a penis cage by a strict, experienced mistress? You want to know how it feels to give up control to a Femdom and put your pleasure in her hands? To be dominated, punished and humiliated by her? But you're just missing the right Mistress to surrender to? Well, then you've come to the right place.

In this book I use you as my personal chastity belt slave. I personally guide you on your way and give you interactive tasks. I'll also help you endure the seven days in the penis cage with proven tips and tricks. Are you strong enough for this challenge, slave?

Exchange of Slaves

Domina Lady Sas is a private Mistress from Frankfurt in Germany. After her first book "Suddenly Dominatrix", where she describes her first steps, she now reports as an experienced and strict Mistress about a very special game. She exchanges slaves with the attractive, sadistic Lady Judith in a hotel in Hamburg. Lady Sas is now in control of the beautiful slavegirl Lisa. And Lady Judith can dominate und use slave Toytoy. In her report Lady Sas shares the night in a very open and frank way.

"Cuckold Stories: Bittersweet humiliations from Lady Sas"

Lady Sas has compiled eight hot cuckold stories that will put a knowing smile on the lips of cuckolds, hotwifes and bulls. Cuckolding is a wonderful game of desires and longings, of jealousy, seduction and breaking taboos. It is highly emotional and excitingly sexy.

200 Ideas for BDSM Sessions. Femdom – Malesub. Fresh ideas and inspiration for your next session

Fresh impulses and ideas keep every relationship alive and vibrant. The experienced Femdom Lady Sas from Frankfurt/Main has compiled 200 exciting, lustful and erotic ideas for you. Get inspired and use these ideas to make your next session a special highlight.

The 200 ideas are divided into six categories:
1. SessionPlay: Ideas for a classic session between Mistress and slave.
2. Role-playing: Ideas for a different role and setting.
3. MindGames: Psycho games for the brain cinema.
4. Humiliation: Ideas on how to make the slave's cheeks blush with shame.
5. Chastity Control: Ideas for a slave wearing a chastity belt.
6. PartyPlay: Ideas for Femdom parties or games with several Femdoms.

"It was very enjoyable to read and you have some amazing and creative ideas :) You have given me some lovely lifestyle ideas!" – Domina Liza, UK

Bonus

"Suddenly Domina – my secret life as a private domina"

Chapter 1: Back to the beginning.

"SEVENTEEN!!!!!!"

"EIGHTEEN!!!!!"

"NINETEEN!!!!!"

"TWENTY!!!!!!"

"TWENTY-ONE!!!!"

"That's enough for now," I remark casually, and spare him the next stroke. Toytoy's ass clearly bears the mark of my whip, glowing bright and red, as we admire our handiwork.

Together, we untie him. He instinctively falls to the floor and showers Cornelitas' vinyl boots and my leather high heels with alternate kisses to express his gratitude.

"You'd better do it properly, or we'll tie you up again..." I snap. "And don't forget my heel, slave."

"The harsher you treat them, the more submissive they become," Cornelitas observes with a smile.

"It's interesting that you mention that," I reply. "I've noticed the same thing."

"I'm disappointed with you, slave," Cornelitas says firmly, as she looks down on Toytoy, who's still submissively kissing and licking our footwear. "I really expected more from you. You're like a little sissy girl that can't take any pain. You're just a snivelling little whiner: 'Please, Lady Cornelitas...! Mercy, Madame, mercy...! I beg you...! Please Lady Cornelitas...' — "Your constant moaning and begging for mercy was simply embarrassing. Very embarrassing, indeed!"

I look at Cornelitas in surprise. She is twisting the facts to suit herself! It's an interesting technique.

"Aren't you ashamed to be such a wimp? You couldn't even take five strokes without complaining. That's pathetic! What an embarrassment you are."

"Please forgive me, Mistress," Toytoy begs with clenched teeth and a hint of irony in his voice. He clearly feels provoked. He had taken his beating bravely and now Cornelitas is claiming that he hadn't.

"What's that?! Do I hear resentment and rebellion in your voice? Kneel, slave!"

She takes a quick step forward and lets loose a shower of slaps on Toytoy, as he cowers before her. Then she quickly steps back again and offers him her boot.

Toytoy immediately obeys, and shows his submission by obediently kissing and licking her shining footwear.

"You seem a bit rebellious sometimes, slave! Am I right?"

"Yes, Lady Cornelitas. Please forgive me, Lady Cornelitas," Toytoy replies in the same defiant voice.

"Behave!" I hiss angrily. "Remember what I told you!"

"Don't worry," Cornelitas reassures me, "we both understand each other very well. We're just playing — aren't we, slave? Oh, I still have some dirt on my shoe..." She points to her heel.

"I need to go to the bathroom," Cornelitas says and winks at me.

"It's over there," I reply and point in that direction.

She laughs. "What I wanted to say was: Has your slave been trained for toilet service?"

"Ehem... not yet," I reply hesitantly. Toilet service? That can't actually be what I think it is, I wonder.

"I understand," says Cornelitas. She takes hold of his leash and pulls Toytoy close to her.

"Would it be beyond your limits if I would piss down on you, slave?" — Yes, she actually uses the word 'piss'.

Toytoy shakes his head.

"Good!" Cornelitas says triumphantly. "Because that is exactly what I intend to do!"

Still holding his leash, she walks assertively to the bathroom, dragging Toytoy behind her. I really want to follow, but somehow don't have the courage to do so.

As if she could read my mind, Cornelitas calls out to me: "You can come and watch, Saskia – if you want to."

I pull myself together and follow them to the bathroom.

My slave is kneeling in the shower.

"Would you mind if I release him from his chastity?" asks Cornelitas. I nod in agreement and give her the key. She unlocks his CB6000, removes all the parts and places them carefully on the bathroom cabinet. Then she lifts her skirt and removes her panties. As I watch, I sense a tingling feeling in my pussy.

Cornelitas stands over the slave and spreads her legs. She places her hands on her hips and asks him: "Have you ever been pissed on, slave?"

To my great surprise, I hear him reply: "Yes, Lady Cornelitas."

"Aha! And who was it who pissed on you?"

"Eh... it happened when I visited some professional femdom studios," Toytoy answers hesitantly.

Without warning, Cornelitas slaps him hard across the face. Or, to judge by the sound it might be more appropriate to say that she whacks him.

"I asked you WHO peed on you, not WHERE," she rebukes him imperiously.

"By Miss Emelie... Lady Silvana de Maart... Lady Pia... Lady Silvia..."

"Aha!" Cornelitas exclaims, "so you're an experienced studio slave. And you like to let ladies piss on you. Do you also drink their piss?"

My slave shakes his head.

"Does Lady Saskia use you as her toilet?"

Again, my slave shakes his head — and my head turns red with embarrassment.

"Would you like her to use you as her toilet?" Cornelitas continues.

Toytoy nods. Wow! My mind races as I take in what I have just learned.

"So you want to feel Lady Saskia's warm nectar on your body? You want to be her dirty little piss-pot?"

Again Toytoy nods in agreement.

"Answer me," Cornelitas says and whacks him across the face a second time.

"Yes, Lady Cornelitas."

"And would you like to take her champagne in your mouth? Would you like to drink her golden nectar like a dirty, greedy little pig?"

"No, Madame."

I am relieved to hear that.

"But if she ordered you to do this for her, would you drink her champagne?"

"Yes, Madame."

"Well spoken," Cornelitas says and gently strokes his cheek. "That is very obedient of you."

"So, would you also drink my piss if I ordered you to do so, slave?"

"No, Madame."

Cornelitas laughs loudly.

"I like you," she says and gently strokes his head. "You have a good sense of humour. But now it's time for a serious answer: Would you also swallow my piss, slave?"

Toytoy shakes his head insistently. "I'm afraid not, Lady Cornelitas."

I feel the tension in the air. How would Cornelitas react to this provocation?

"You do understand that today I am also your Mistress, slave?"

"Yes, Lady Cornelitas, but drinking pee is really one of my taboos", Toytoy explains.

"Aha... but you are still willing to swallow Lady Saskia's pee, so it isn't really a taboo? Or did I miss something?"

"Yes, Lady Cornelitas"

"Are you saying that you don't like me?" Cornelitas' voice is no longer as calm as it was earlier. She sounds offended.

"I like you very much, Madame."

"Aha. And why should I believe you?" She looks at Toytoy inquiringly. "Very well. Enough small talk. Take your pathetic cock and jerk it for me... yes... show me how big it can get... very good... watch out, it's about to come..."

She stands over the slave, who is jerking his cock faster and faster.

I stand by the door and observe the scene. My thoughts start to wander. And I think back to how everything began. Toytoy and I are in an SM relationship. The abbreviation "SM" sounds harmless. Like "WC", "TV" or "ABS". However, when it is spelled out as "sadism and masochism" it has a very different ring. And that is precisely what it means. In this book I would like to tell the story of how I became what I am today: a private dominatrix.

At the end of this book I have added a glossary that explains some important concepts from the world of BDSM. Uninitiated readers can look up the meaning of specialist terms that are used in the text. For example:

BDSM —

Abbreviation for bondage and discipline, dominance and submission, sadism and masochism.

(...)

(End of Excerpt)

Impressum

Femdom Academy

By Lady Sas

February 2021

Upated August 2023

Frankfurt/Main, Germany

Contact: dearladysas@gmail.com

Lady-Sas.com

Illustration: Shutterstock

Code: 39 61 24

Made in United States
Troutdale, OR
11/26/2024

25350590R00144